AT ALL TIMES, IN EVERY AGE

Father Eusebe M. Menard

Rev. Francis R. Davis
Our Lady Of Lourdes
120 Fairmont Road
Elmira, N. Y. 14905

AT ALL TIMES, IN EVERY AGE

Father Eusebe M. Menard

FRANCISCAN HERALD PRESS
1434 West 51st Street
Chicago, Illinois 60609

At All Times, In Every Age by Eusebe M. Menard, translated by Paul Schwartz from the French **A Toute Heure** published by the author. Rights and permission granted by the author. Copyright © 1977 by Franciscan Herald Press, 1434 West 51st Street, Chicago, Illinois 60609. Made in the United States.

Library of Congress Cataloging in Publication Data:
Menard, Eusebe M.
  At all times, in every age.

  Translation of A toute heure.
  1. Catholic Church—Clergy. 2. Christian life—Catholic authors. 3. Christianity—20th century.
I. Title.
BX1912.M4613	248'.48'2	77-23466
ISBN 0-8199-0663-8

Nihil Obstat:
  E. Boisvert O.F.M.

Imprimi Potest:
  P. Luc-Marie Chabot O.F.M.

Imprimatur:
  E. Berard V.E.

September 18, 1967

"The Nihil Obstat and Imprimatur are official declarations that a book or pamphlet is free of doctrinal error. No indication is contained therein that those who have granted the Nihil Obstat and Imprimatur agree with the contents, opinions, or statements expressed."

MADE IN THE UNITED STATES OF AMERICA

I would like to offer my heartfelt thanks to Father Thivollier for his kind assistance in the editing of this work.

Eusèbe M. Ménard

PREFACE

Our world is rushing into the unknown with dizzying, uncontrollable speed. It is anxious for change and fearful that time is short. Man, though he is himself the agent of the changes, finds himself so whirled along by them that he now faces an identification crisis. He is filled with distress and cries out in anguish for immediate answers.

Contemporary man sees himself as living his entire life, willingly or unwillingly, in bondage to many things and persons that determine the range of his experience and force him into action that is often the impersonal action of the crowd. Politics, economics, social conditions, relations among men, even the experience of God or of his absence are all influenced by the constant change going on in the society we have built. Man is ever anxious to find new values in society, but the pressure of time, work, and change itself leaves him without the leisure required for the quest, for meditation, for a balanced approach to things.

Absorbed by work and by the headlong onward rush of the world; man, wherever he turns, is plagued by the "absence of God," so much so that he has raised this absence to the dignity of an "existential category" special to our time. God seems not to be present in his world, yet today as never before man appears to long for God. He asks: How real is God today? Can he love me, can I love him? Does he know me, can I know him?

Hidden in the answers to these questions is the concept of authentic conversion to God, that is so evangelical and so much needed today.

"To be converted" today means to encounter the personal God who is at work in the world, in a new fashion, through the signs of the times. "To encounter" him is to be reconciled to this God who lives in man's today which is also the today of God.

The whole process presupposes reflection, personal renewal, and a great deal of faith. Given such faith, the very anxiety for the search paradoxically disposes to conversion as understood according to the Gospel (see Acts 14:15; 26:18; John 6:44; Luke 7:50; 15:17). "There is one among you whom you do not recognize," turn to him! says the Baptist (John 1:26).

Once Christ, the Word of the Father, became incarnate, we discover the God who is the goal of conversion, only if we start with man "Once it has thus been drawn into, indeed incarnated in, a dialogue with God, man's existence in this world becomes an anonymous revelation when we get into the area of religious meaning" (Schillebeeckx). The Incarnation turns the whole of history into a history of salvation, in which God is personally present and active. He is seemingly invisible, yet we can find him and know him so as to love him and be converted to him. Then he is really the focus of our life, when we view life as the act in which we encounter, experience, and are reconciled with the Father.

The youth of today

The present generation of young people stands aghast at the spiritual state of our century. This is the century of the machine, of production and consumption, of the reification of man and the pollution of the environment, of hunger and war; the century in which men act like machines and machines act like men. At the same time, it is by contrast a century of brilliant thinkers, of progress, and of art; a time when life is beautiful and men are filled with a yearning to love and be loved. This is the century young people find so disconcerting, but they adopt divergent positions and attitudes toward the situation.

The young people of today are astounded to see the material rhythm of the world becoming ever quicker, while men are spiritually unable to achieve the balance needed if they are not to become self-destructive monsters.

Many in their confusion have turned to solutions that are likewise imbalanced: drugs, lethargic idleness, promiscuity, and suicide. Perhaps they sought and did not find the right leader who could enlighten them and give them the strength to put their ideas into practice or to create outlets for their generosity and bring alive for themselves the true values that create a balance between the material and the spiritual.

At the same time, however, there are many, very many other young people who combine generosity, courage, and energy in the struggle to effect an extraordinary change in the world. These young people are the hope of the world, though they may annoy us at times when in their desperate sincerity they accuse us of having built a world that neither enjoys material things nor has any interior life, a world both perfect and fictitious, a world that has developed the mass media yet is filled with a terrible psychological loneliness, a world that creates for the future and despairs of the present.

Without this youthful spirit of fiery sincerity, all hopes are stillborn. It is vitally necessary for us that the young should go on protesting and being intolerant. They can restore our joy in living and our ability to imagine, to change things, to be optimists and idealists, to be "someone" in human society and not just something that is useful. Young people do not buy happiness; they create it, they produce it and live it. Adults who create and produce we regard as geniuses; the rest of us, the majority, go along with the status quo or buy an escape into artificial joy.

Young people who are alert and alive can teach us to be spontaneously productive, to meditate, to create, to live joyously. If we can combine our adult experience with the creative energy of youth, we will be able to pursue an "ideal" that is concrete, and live a "commitment" that is authentic. These will motivate our lives and give direction to our existence. Only thus will we be able to find and maintain the spiritual rhythm, the hope human and divine, the love and the balance of which the world stands so much in need today.

If all this is to happen, we need a leader who stands apart from the mass, a guide, someone who understands human life and lives a divine life.

Need of a spiritual leader

Contemporary society is filled with the absence of God. It wears the blinkers of scientism and is so clever at explaining everything in terms of the world system rather than by divine intervention. It is alive with earthbound messianism and shot through with the spirit of secularism that believes the evangelical spirit to be worthless in making up for man's lack of maturity. The secularist mind regards God as a useless hypothesis and seeks to apply technology to the intrahuman world. Such a society needs a spiritual leader who can restore it to intimacy with the living God and enable the man in the street to discover how marvelously the personal God is at work in our world.

When confronted with the world, man needs effective guidance if he is to discover the immensely great God who invites him to rise above himself, to go out of himself and enter into familiarity with this God.

Such a spiritual leader is par excellence the priest, the man who has vital experience of his own times and is chosen from among his fellows to lead the people of God toward the invisible. Being part of his world, today's priest may himself be a victim of the confusion abroad in the world, because his faith can no longer be based on certainties shared by those around him. He is not a clairvoyant and does not know how the world will turn out. Yet at this critical juncture he is endowed with the charisms men need today, and he follows the invisible road as though he could see Christ, for he is following the word of Christ.

A difficult task indeed, and one that the priest can carry out only to the extent that he is filled with the word of God, lives it, and prays over it, and to the extent that at the same time, he lives amid the reality of today's world.

The priest must, by means of the word, be on the watch for the action of grace and discern it amid the hurly-burly of life. He is attuned to the signs of the times that mark the today of God, to the life of the people and the signals emitted by the word of God that has taken concrete shape in the people of God. He learns to hear the signals the word gives, for only thus can he safely guide the people. The word of God, after all, yields certainty, for it is the way, the truth, and the life. Once he has heard the word, he embarks upon activity that is human, yet has a divine depth; activity that is organized, community-oriented, Eucharistic; the activity of social and religious commitment, of witness and poverty. The spiritual leader builds solely in the name and on the word of Jesus (Luke 5:5, 10).

A spirituality of love

All this presupposes a personal commitment and spirituality that are sufficiently comprehensive and profound to be an authentic response to the restless seeking of contemporary man.

Our age will accept as a leader only the person who can reconcile love of God and love of the world, the ascetical effort to practice renunciation and the human effort to advance, develop, and change.

The man of today, who reflects God in his life by continuing God's creative work, needs someone who will wholeheartedly help him to unite his will to the will of God and to bring his heart into harmony with the heart of God in all he does.

The man of today is in love with his world, yet at the same time feels a confusion of mind that is produced by the dizzying pace of change in that world. He longs to love God in a way that is personal yet also involves the community, and that is fully conscious and free.

The spiritual leader of today must be able to respond to contemporary man's need, by showing even the man in the street that the heart of Christ is a source of fruitful energy and an incarnation of that thrust toward God that he desires for himself. The heart of Christ must be shown to be living and accessible, for the dynamism of love is fully manifest there, and the interpersonal love between man and God that Christ embodies proves to be the fulfillment of the lofty aspirations of contemporary man. The fleshly, Eucharistic heart of Christ, a heart that finds expression in his life and daily work, makes the response that contemporary man so much desires to make as he turns wholeheartedly to the God he finds present in his own life and concerned for his own life.

Today then, the priestly mission, based on the spirituality of the Sacred Heart, is more than ever a redemptive mission, a Christocentric mission, an eschatological mission (1 Cor. 15:28; Col. 3:11; Eph. 4:10).

These various reflections fit in perfectly with the essence of priesthood as theology sees it. For the priest is the mediator, before the Father and in Christ's name, for the ecclesial community to which he belongs.

As mediator, he belongs to both of the worlds he brings together. He must sum up in himself, as it were, the lives and problems of men, and then be able to go a step further and, through his ecclesial life, actions, and words help establish a harmony, a shared orientation, between the life of the man in the street and the Lord. Such a harmony does not lead to a temporal messianism nor, at the other extreme, to confronting the world as a kind of prosecutor; it means rather, allowing grace to play its life giving role in daily action.

To this end the priest must be at home with the problems of his world, the problems whose scope we mentioned above. At the same time, he must be at home in the life of God so that he may help his people grasp the Gospel message in relation to their daily lives. The priest must link human experience to the plan of God as manifested in the word of Christ and seen at work in human life when the latter is viewed in the light of the revealed and incarnate Word. The priest must be able to draw into vital unity all that is most human with all that is most Christic. Through his own discovery of the divine message that is contained in the Word, he has to be able to draw together Christ and his poor, the Lord and his people.

The priest sees to it that through the Eucharist and a vibrant ceremonial the people of God learns experientially how the whole of its life is vitally united to the Lord at the altar. With the priest's help all of us need to discover that behind the Bread and Wine there is not only a sacrament and a sacrifice, but the human Christ uniting himself to the Father, in our name and with our words, in an eternal covenant, and taking with him into that covenant our human attitudes and our human lives. The priest must understand, and authentically live in accordance with, the values of the contemporary world and the signs of God in contemporary life; he must unite all of them to the Sacrament, so that Christ may ever more fully glorify the Father through these values, this life of ours, and all our activity.

The yearning of contemporary man to give all things a new vitality and a spiritual dimension means that our need is greater than ever before of priests who are more fully human, more fully men of our age. They must be adults, not children, when it comes to faith; they must have intimate experience of God, the Eucharist, and revealed truth.

The cry of Jeremiah still echoes today: "The people ask for bread, but there is no one to give it to them." Only the kind of priest we have been describing can reply, as Isaiah did, "Here I am, send me!"

Dear reader, if this Preface has stirred your interest, you will certainly be anxious to plunge into the book Father Ménard has given us on the priesthood and on the call the Lord addresses to us "at every moment." Perhaps the world is now living in the twenty-fifth hour; but even if it is, the Lord will go on calling, and in an age such as ours he will have to find someone apart from the mass to act as his priest.

We are grateful to Father Ménard for his splendid gift, for in this book he makes us see that the presence of the Lord in our age depends on us. We must be generous and answer "Yes" to life and "Yes" to the Lord.

Luis Cordero

Dr. Luis Cordero is Professor of Cultural Anthropology, Scientific Research, and Law in the Pontifical and Civil Faculty of Theology at Lima.

PRESENTATION

Over the course of the last thirty-five years, Father E. Ménard, the author of the present volume, has traveled through city and country — a little like a St. Francis or a St. Bernard — inviting young people and adults to listen within themselves for a call to do more with their lives. He has been an eloquent spokesman for this Word addressed to men and women and will never know how great has been the response he has been able to inspire on this road. It would be no exaggeration, however, to say that thousands of persons — including the author of this introduction — have chosen to commit themselves in the steps of Christ after hearing his call through the voice of Father Ménard.

A man of action, Father Ménard has tried to be consistent with the message he preaches. Since 1945 not only has he established training centers for young people and adults interested in a Christian commitment in several countries, but he has also founded two religious communities for men and women with the same goal. He and his followers have been active in Canada, the United States, Latin America and Africa.

In 1956 Father Ménard founded a seminary for adult vocations, Holy Apostles College in Cromwell, Connecticut. The college is directed and staffed by the Missionaries of the Holy Apostles (another foundation of Father Ménard), a Roman Catholic religious society whose goal is to train religious leaders, both clerical and lay, which the universal church needs for its service among the poor.

As if word and deed were not enough for Father Ménard to achieve his goals, he has also tried to make use of the written word. In spite of his many activities, he has several volumes to his credit which are all directly or indirectly concerned with the one call he never ceases to proclaim.

In the present book he speaks primarily to young readers from twenty to thirty-five who do not yet have a definite career or who are interested in making a change. They are invited to become aware of the necessity and worth of the sacramental ministry in God's plan of salvation for men.

But it would narrow the scope of this book to suggest that it is addressed only to future priests. For it is a fact that even during the era of the hierarchical church, Father Ménard sparked many to Christian involvement outside clerical structures through his pastoral work.

Even so, we can hope that in our secularized world of today this book of Father Ménard's will awaken an interest in the priesthood among many. In any case, we can be sure that it will provoke in all its readers a greater effort to assist in the spreading and the *living* of the gospel message, according to each one's possibilities.

"At all times," to be sure, the Lord gives me a sign, calls me to his service. What he asks of me might seem to be less impressive than what he asks another. But that doesn't matter. What matters is that I make an effort every day to hear this Word within me; and that having heard it, I make it my life.

"Today let us close not our hearts, but attend to the voice of the Lord!"

                        Roland-Jules Doucet

                        Director of Adult Education
                        St. John Vianney College
                        Montreal, Canada

April, 1976

TABLE OF CONTENTS

Preface	vii
Presentation	xiii
Introduction	1

PART ONE

I.	Problems of Their Day and Age	4
	Reflections	9
II.	Meeting Christ	10
	Reflections	11
III.	The New Age, The New Creation	12
IV.	The New Kingdom	14
	Reflections	19
V.	Fishers of Men	25
	Reflection	31

PART TWO

I.	Renewal for All	32
II.	Temptations of the Kingdom	37
	Reflections	42
III.	The Least of the Servants	45
	Reflections	47
IV.	For All Peoples, All Places, All Times	49
V.	The Sacrifice of the Cross	53
	Reflections	56

VI.	The Risen Christ	61
	Reflections — *The Waters of Baptism*	64
	The Pardon of Sinners	66
	The Sacrifice of Calvary	73
	The Eucharist: One Heart, One Spirit	76
	The Universal Celebration	78

PART THREE

I.	Come One, Come All	80
	Reflections	83
II.	In Spite of Their Faults	87
	Reflections	94
III.	To Take Up the Cross	97
	1. *The Companions of Jesus and Money*	97
	2. *The Companions of Jesus and Bonds of the Heart*	99
	3. *The Companions of Jesus and Life in a Group*	101
	4. *The Companions of Jesus and Total Commitment*	105
	Reflections	106
	1. *Poverty*	106
	2. *Celibacy*	108
	3. *Life in Community*	111
	4. *A Life Given Without Reserve*	118
IV.	The Joy in Jesus' Call	120
	Reflections	121

INTRODUCTION

**The hours slide across the ancient sundial...
The time is always ripe for hearing a new call.**

The time of the harvest had come. And the ripe grapes, all swollen with sun and nectar, lay waiting day in and day ou, in constant danger of being lost, of drying up or rotting on the vine; waiting for the harvesters to gather them and carry them to the cellars of abundance.

The master of the vineyard knew this and was attentive.

One morning he went out at dawn to hire some laborers. In the square at the center of town he found dayworkers who had come for the harvest. He agreed on a wage with them, perhaps a piece of silver, and sent them into his vineyard.

Since these first workers weren't enough, he came back around nine o'clock in the morning looking for men still without work and said to them, "You go into my vineyard too, and I'll pay you a just wage, according to your hours of labor." And they went.

But the harvest turned out to be so abundant that even more hands were needed. Around noon and again about three hours later the master of the vineyard came back to the hiring place. He was sure he would find the workers he needed. In fact, when he first planted his vine he knew that there would never be any lack of laborers in his country; if so, he would have never undertaken such a vast planting. He once again found people ready to work and sent them into his vineyard.

Meanwhile, the day grew older. And undoubtedly some storm or another was threatening or some devastating cloud of locusts was advancing. The harvest had to be safe in the cellars before nightfall at all costs.

The shadow of the sundial read five hours past noon when the master of the vineyard returned to the square and found some men unoccupied:

"How is it that you have stayed here all day doing nothing?"

"Well, no one has hired us."

Were they too timid to go looking for work? Or did they think they wouldn't make good harvesters and gave up all hope?

But the master, a good judge of men, sized them up differently: "Go ahead; you go work in my vineyard also."

Heeding his call in spite of the late hour, they left in great haste for the harvest of the ripe grapes.

After the day had ended, the master of the vineyard said to his foreman:

"Call the harvesters and give them their agreed wage, starting with those who came last."

The latecomers each received one piece of silver, the same as those who had worked since sunrise. The last men were understandably somewhat jealous. But the master has another way of seeing things. What counts for him is the harvest gathered in his cellars; without it, everything — or almost everything — would be lost. He is happy and wants everyone who participated in saving the harvest to have a share in his joy, whether they spent many or few hard hours in the sun, had more or less know-how, showed greater or lesser zeal in the final hours.

Think about it: There was much worry and fear during the day; but because everyone responded to the call, tonight the entire harvest rests in great vats in the immense cellar. All are invited to the same rejoicing. How good and overflowing will be the wine of the wedding feast in this kingdom!

And you, reader and friend, perhaps it's you that the master of the vineyard of humanity wants to see at the hiring-place sometime today; you who have already spent

The reader can find this story in the Gospel of Matthew, chapter 20 (verses 1 to 16).

some 17, 18, 25 or more years on this earth.

Perhaps in reading through the pages which follow you will hear a call; or perhaps a call you have already heard will become even clearer.

Don't shut your heart, don't harden yourself with resistance as if this book were an intruder — at least not without having run through a few of these pages. Don't let the chance to answer slip through your fingers: "If you really want me, Lord, I'm ready to follow you."

If God allows our planet to carry over three billion people in our day, you can be sure that he has also made plans for a proportionate call of at least one million apostles and priests. Perhaps you are one of them.

The harvest of souls is waiting for you. The gathering-in of men is in danger of perishing for want of laborers, like the ripe grapes on the hillsides.

PART ONE

chapter one

Problems of Their Day and Age

There was once a group of friends and courageous fishermen on Lake Galilee: Andrew, John, Simon, James and several others. They really enjoyed their work and got together in a small association which owned their fishing boats and huge nets, and hired extra help.

Life on the lake had its risks. Sometimes they would spend the entire night out there, letting out their nets in order to encircle a school of fish, but without any catch whatever to show for their efforts. They also had to endure terrible storms; the great lake surrounded by hills was known for its tempestuous winds capable of swamping a boat. But then sometimes the catch was good; after selling their take at daybreak, the men would be busy the rest of the day repairing the nets that had torn under the strain of the heavy catch.

Yet their work did not absorb them to the point that they forgot the great problems of their people and their time.

Opening To The World Of Tomorrow Through A Close Reading Of The Prophets.

Familiar with the reading of the prophets since their childhood, they nourished in the bottom of their hearts their hopes for a better world where the rich and the powerful would no longer exploit the poor and the powerless; where the ignorant would be taught; where the sick and the crippled would finally be consoled, cared for, and cured; where prisons would no longer exist because they had become useless; where the people would no longer see itself crushed, betrayed, sold by its leaders, delivered into slavery, or sent into exile; where the country itself would be liberated, recover its independence (they then lived under a Roman army of occupation), and find its own place among all the other nations and races on the earth.

Their trade and their life was fishing on Lake Galilee, but they were even more interested in the problems of their country and their day.

They were waiting for the liberator promised by the prophets, the Messiah who would inaugurate a new "golden age," a new system of social life where men, as the prophet Isaiah foretold some 700 years earlier, instead of treating one another like ferocious and dangerous beasts, would live in friendship in a climate of perpetual peace, help, and understanding; a social system where man would no longer act like a wolf toward his fellow man, and would not behave with the ferocity of a panther, the pretention of a lion lording over it all, the meanness of a bear clawing and ripping, the wiliness of a cobra or a viper striking at the imprudent hand of the innocent.

They knew the famous words of the prophet proclaiming not only the replacement of the law of the jungle by the law of love but also the great change which would follow in human living. He spoke of this change as it would be reflected among the animals:

> The wolf lives with the lamb,
> the panther lies down with the kid,
> calf and lion cub feed together
> with a little boy to lead them.
> The cow and the bear make friends,
> their young lie down together.
> The lion eats straw like the ox.

This text, one of the most famous in the whole bible, can be found in chapter 2 of the Book of the prophet Isaiah.

The infant plays over the cobra's hole;
into the viper's lair
the young child puts his hand.
They do no hurt, no harm...
for the country is filled with the knowledge of God
as the waters swell the sea.

Meeting At The River On the Edge Of The Desert, Gathering Around The Teacher: John The Baptist.

To keep this hope and this vision alive in their hearts, and to better prepare themselves for the immanent arrival of the Messiah who would inaugurate this new state of things, the men from Lake Galilee gathered, between two fishing seasons, around a new prophet who sprang up out of the desert: John the Baptist they called him. They became fervent disciples of this new "forerunner" who saw himself as the "echoing voice" of the great prophet Isaiah.

John the Baptist's entry on the scene is reported in the gospels: chapter 3 of Matthew, chapter 1 of Mark, and chapter 3 of Luke.

John lived in the uninhabited plains alongside the river Jordan. He was a man of the desert: limbs and torso all leathered from long years of life under the sun. His only clothing a kind of loincloth woven from camel's hair, held up around his waist by a leather belt, and his only food the kind furnished by desolate regions like these: roasted locusts, wild honey and cakes of barley or rye.

Far from the noise of the cities, the prophet could hear God speaking to him in the depths of his heart. And perhaps he was a member of the group of monks at Qumran whose precious manuscripts were discovered in the famous caves alongside the Dead Sea. These men, cut off from the world, divided their time between study and prayer in the hope of the Messiah, persuaded their life of penance would hasten his coming.

Obeying a mysterious call, the Baptist came to the banks of the Jordan to proclaim the immanent coming of the Messiah.

He compared himself to the herald who precedes a royal procession: "Prepare the triumphal path! Make straight the curves, level out the bumps, fill in the holes!" He was speaking in a figurative sense: the road to be prepared was in the heart of each man and woman.

Andrew, Simon, John, James and the others heard the Baptist talk about turning their lives around, with all that that implied. For he wanted them to start thinking about what they were doing about social justice and how they were concerned for the poor: those without money, without bread, without homes, ill-clothed, powerless, unliked, etc. All this was nothing new, but came straight from the ancient prophets who wrote in their day:

> All your religious ceremonies
> are great, splendid;
> But they fill God with horror,
> and weigh upon his heart.
> You have multiplied your prayers,
> but he closes his ears.
> Your hands he sees covered with blood
> (innocent blood).
> Go, wash yourselves:
> make your hearts clean.
> Despise wrong-doing;
> make your break with evil,
> learn to do good.
> Search for justice,
> run to help the oppressed,
> protect the rights of the orphan,
> plead for the poor widow.
> Then, after that, you can come
> before me (says God) and
> we will talk this over.
> Even if your souls are
> red with sins,
> and your hands crimson with blood,
> they shall be white as snow... .

The Baptist could also recall the words of the prophet Isaiah:

> The penitence I like, God has told you, is this:
> to break unjust chains
> undo the bonds of the yoke
> to let the oppressed go free
> and break every oppression,
> to share your bread with the hungry
> to shelter the homeless poor
> to clothe the man you see naked
> and not turn from your own kin.

The Book of the prophet Isaiah, chapter 58.

Then your light will rise in the darkness...
The Lord will respond to your calls,
for he is full of mercy... .

To all those who came to ask his advice — "What do I have to do to get ready for the coming of the Messiah, to become worthy to stand at his side for his total renewal of the world?" — the Baptist answered very clearly that the most urgent thing was to practice justice and the love of one's neighbor, and not so much to leave one's normal routine, one's business or way of life.

But for most people that meant some kind of change in their life. And it was good that those who were firmly resolved should indicate this by a meaningful, decisive act which committed and involved them in front of everyone else. The Baptist pointed to the river. Then these men and women publicly confessed their faults, took off their sandals and their robes, and went down into the river. And the Baptist poured water on every head which emerged from the river, as a sign of purification and renewal.

Overcome by the man and his teaching, the fishermen from the Sea of Galilee were getting ready to join the troops of the Messiah that the Baptist said had come, but who still lived in hiding. In any case, they were ready to abandon their jobs and risk any adventure for such a great cause.

REFLECTIONS

You Who Dream A Tomorrow Full Of Song And Build The Year 2000...

...you would not be reading these pages if you did not cherish a great ideal at the bottom of your heart and were you not filled with the desire to share it with those around you.

Like these fishermen of Galilee — Andrew, Simon, John, James and the others — the job you are doing, the studies you undertake, the family which you perhaps dream of having one day and for which you are getting ready — these things don't make you forget the great problems of your city, your land or your time.

Those men fed themselves on reading the prophets, and liked to listen to the Baptist on the banks of the River Jordan. But you too have your leaders; you nourish yourself on their teachings. We're not talking here about their philosophies, their social or political theories; for these can be different or even in conflict. But what is certain is that some men and women have a seductive power over you and the young people of your time. They fill you with enthusiasm, and you march behind them resolved to work with all your strength for the coming of "tomorrows filled with song."

You want things to change in the world; you want the "law of the jungle" which too often stands between men to give way to the law of love.

You are building the year 2000. All kinds of meetings, articles in the newspapers and magazines, and radio and television programs are opening to worldwide perspectives. Maybe you are a member of a youth group, a union, a charitable organization. You perhaps take part in demonstrations, or even in a struggle for great causes: peace, world hunger, literacy programs for the unschooled, the eradication of miserable slums, or the like.

And it could be that you too like to go back from time to time "to the desert" in some retreat house to reflect and pray there.

In short, you are looking for a way to situate your life so that it will be a personal achievement and will serve the advancement of other persons and peoples.

Believe me, you are a lot like Andrew, Simon, John, James and the others, the fishermen from Galilee, when they were being fed on their reading of the prophets and left to find the Baptist on the banks of the Jordan, at the edge of the desert... .

chapter two
Meeting Christ

The fishermen from Galilee were the first to have the experience: meeting Christ is both amazing and very simple.

One beautiful day a man named Jesus of Nazareth presented himself on the banks of the Jordan. The Baptist, pointing him out to John and Andrew, made this unexpected pronouncement: "Look closely at this man; it's him, the Messiah — it's him, the Christ!"

Andrew and John, not doubting the word of the prophet for a minute, left him in order to follow this mysterious person at a respectful distance.

He, seeing that they were following him, turned around: "What do you want?"

"Master, where do you live?" they timidly replied, hoping for his attention — and another meeting.

"Come with me and you'll see."

The Gospel of the apostle John, chapter 1 (verses 35 to 50).

They went with him. This was in the afternoon, about four o'clock. They spent the whole evening together, speaking very casually with him.

We can imagine all kinds of things about this first meeting. What was it really like? The gospels are always silent about this and reveal little about what happened in these hearts meeting Jesus for the first time.

But we do know that Andrew and John were quickly overcome. The next day it was hardly dawn before Andrew went looking for his brother Simon to share his new discovery: "Simon! Great news! We've found the Messiah!"

And he brought him to Jesus. For his part, John altered his brother James. Then Phillip heard the news and brought along his friend Bartholomew-Nathaniel.

Jesus, knowing men's hearts, judged them quickly. Simon, the chief of their small fishing group, he renamed "Peter" or "the Rock." As for Bartholomew-Nathaniel, who was a little skeptical because he didn't think anything worthwhile could come out of the little village of Nazareth, Jesus showed him that he read the depths of men's hearts and that in spite of the distance he knew the man's reactions when Phillip went to get him. He even said that it all happened under a fig tree. Bartholomew-Nathaniel couldn't get over it; he remained confused. But Jesus told them that they were only beginning their discoveries; for they would see much more.

REFLECTIONS

You've Heard About Christ; And What Have You Discovered? A Doctrinal System? A Moral Code? Or A Companion For Your Road?

While you were learning about all the great men in history, one day someone undoubtedly told you about Jesus. You've heard different things about him, for the life and activities of his disciples are sufficiently well-known to the world so that some question has at least passed through your head. You have probably even learned about his life and studied his teachings, his doctrine, or his ethics.

But Jesus himself, as a living person, as a travelling companion with whom you speak easily all evening — did you discover him one day, meet him, with a feeling of warm presence deep in your heart?

Think hard; it would have been on an occasion which was going to mark and change your life. It was in hearing a friend speak, watching him live, moving along with him. It was connected with some book, some conference, a day of reflection. "Where do you live, Lord?" "Come with me, and you'll see."

And quickly you understood that with him there was no hiding yourself because our hearts are naked before him and he reads the darkest depths of our conscience as if it were in full light of day. But he's come to take to the road with us, not to judge or condemn. He knows what's inside man and yet he wants to need us. And he really trusts us!

chapter three

The New Age, The New Creation

To inaugurate the new age, water changed into wine at a village wedding announced the transformation of all creation.

Jesus had told Peter, Andrew, John, James, Phillip, Bartholomew, and the others that they were only beginning their discoveries. And in fact they were soon going to see the one who came to begin a "new age" on earth at work. A significant event was going to prove it.

This account is taken from chapter 2 of John's Gospel.

A couple of days later they found themselves in the small town of Cana where the whole village was at a wedding. Cana isn't far from Nazareth, and Mary, Jesus' mother, was among those celebrating. Jesus and his companions, who were traveling through, were thus also invited to join in the rejoicing.

But Mary, who was helping serve the food, was all preoccupied with the success of the feast. She was familiar with the smallest details of the preparations and knew that the wine reserves had run out.

At her request, in order to save the newlyweds and their families from embarrassment and so that no shadow would come to darken the joy of such a beautiful day, Jesus had six great stone jars filled with water; he then changed the water into wine.

This was not only marvellous; it was the commencement of a whole plan. Jesus came to bring about a renewal of the world, a transformation of the whole of creation. Men, too, should be transformed into something utterly new; and how much more noble and fitting than in the image of water changed at a wedding into the best wine of an even better vintage?

And in fact, without waiting any longer, Jesus began to travel around the country, proclaiming the arrival of a new state of affairs: "Change your heart! Change your life! The reign of God has come! It's here. It's already started among you."

The Gospel of the disciple Mark, chapter 1 (verses 14 and 15).

His first companions followed him. For since the marvel of the water changed into wine they began to believe that Jesus was the Messiah they waited for. The crowds trooped after him to hear his message.

What was going on?

Well, a totally new framework of reality was being introduced; a reversal of the scale of values taken for granted by humanity had begun.

In the many nations, among the kingdoms of the earth, the sin of men tended to transform society into a real jungle where self-interest, ambition, strength, violence, lies, and tricks were law. The supreme value, the "standard" for which all strived and against which all were measured, was Money; for money brought power and pleasure.

In the new order it's the other way around: the only value which serves as a standard is Love. No, not just any love, but "loving others in the same love with which God loves them."

And this is why it's called the "reign of God." Men are going to recognize themselves as his children, made in his image; they will respect and love one another as brothers and sisters because they have the same Father. Among them trust, sympathy, and mutual aid will flourish. They will have only one preoccupation: to help one another grow so that each one's life will be fully realized.

This explicit commandment of Christ is found in the Gospel of the apostle John, chapter 13 (verses 34 and 35).

The citizens of this new kingdom? Those who live this law: "Love one another as God loves you." And this region of God knows no borders and breaks through all times and centuries, because it finds its seat in all hearts. It is as vast as the universe, for he who reigns within is the God who fills the worlds with his presence. This kingdom reaches its fulfillment beyond this life on earth; it moves beyond death. To be a "citizen" here is to be sure of the friendship of God for an infinity of time.

chapter four

The New Kingdom

But who will go to proclaim to the world, echoing the voice of Christ, this utter reversal of the scale of values in the new kingdom: "To love others as God has loved me."

The proclamation of the "Beatitudes" is found in Matthew's Gospel, chapter 5 (verses 3 to 12).

So Jesus went through the cities and the countryside announcing this new conception of reality.

But this proclamation is meant to resound through all the universe and down through the centuries as long as there will be men on earth. Who, then, could be the "echoing voice" of Christ, carrying it to the ends of the earth and the end of time?

***

Who will carry this proclamation to those who believe that money creates happiness, that a successful life is measured in terms of one's fortune or status, comfort, good reputation, luck in business or games, in health or in love?

Then who will go out "echoing Christ's voice" to proclaim to these people that you really succeed with your life when you keep your heart both free and open; not in distrusting the things of this earth — for there is no reason to whine about progress or technology or even happiness — but in a detachment from money, satisfactions, privileges and power. You can be unlucky, badly off, gripped by sickness and infirmity, driven to disaster, disliked and taken for granted — and still be successful with your life! Why? Because in spite of all that you were never bitter, disappointed, sour or envious. Your heart remained open and full of love for others; you understood them, loved them, and helped them. You rejoiced with those who were joyful; you wept with those who were weeping. In short, you loved as God loves. So in this new conception of reality you have made it; you have won.

Then who will go to retell the story once told by Jesus about the rich man who piled up a fortune and dreamed of ever bigger warehouses, crying, "I'm on top of the world! From now on I can eat, drink and be merry to my heart's content!" The idiot! The next night he died. How much better off he'd have been to concentrate on values other than money! For "what good is it to gain the world and all its riches," said Jesus, "if this victory costs you your soul!"

The story of the foolish rich man is found in chapter 12 of Luke's Gospel.

...Or to those who think that "might makes right," that life is made for imposing yourself on others, crushing your rivals, destroying your enemies, getting revenge on your adversaries, proving yourself merciless for the weak and conquered since life is a matter of fighting and winning...?

...Then who will proclaim to these people, echoing Christ's voice, this radical turn-around of values: that on the contrary, you live a real life when you have people's respect; when you do not mistreat them, crush them, dirty their reputations; when you know how to forget their mistakes and avoid rancor; when you forgive them from the depths of the heart. "If someone slaps you on your right cheek, turn him your left cheek," said Jesus as he tried to express in a vivid image the idea that it is better to suffer a personal injury, to give more than is required, if that will put an end to hate and its vicious circle of bigotry and violence, if that will stop hearts from going rotten and behaving like enemies.

Each person should say to himself, in short: the rule is to love others as God has loved me. Then how has God loved me? He's loved me in spite of my backsliding and my sins; and even though I was really nothing in his eyes, he forgave me. Then I should give witness to this forgiveness I've received in forgiving others.

Then who will go retell the parable told by Jesus about the heartless steward who owed his master the incredible sum of one and a half million dollars, and who, when confronted with his debt, threw himself at his master's feet and discovered the other's endless goodness, came away forgiven and even, unlikely as it may seem, had his whole debt canceled. Yet before he was even out of the palace, this reprieved and freed steward met one of his subordinates who owed him the insignificant sum of two dollars. The steward jumped for the other's throat and, ignoring his pleas and his promise of repayment in a short time, had him thrown into prison and ordered the confiscation of all his possessions. You can imagine the rage of the master when this reached his ears: "Ingrate! Shouldn't you have pity on your servant as I had pity on you?" And in his indignation he gave him over to the hands of the law. In the same way, concluded Jesus, God will also deal with those who do not forgive from the depths of their heart.

This parable is in chapter 18 of Matthew's Gospel.

...Or to those who think "it's everyone for himself"; that success comes from forgetting about others, not letting yourself get carried away by compassion ("I'm not my brother's keeper"); knowing how to keep your distance from those who don't think the same way as you or who don't share the same interests; building barriers and walls against those who are from another country or of another race or a different color of skin or another mentality or a different class; keeping up your guard and not trusting anyone: "peace is built on strong defenses!"

Then who will go proclaim to these people, echoing the voice of Christ, this radical turn-around of values: that you succeed in life when you become passionately interested in others for their own success, their own advancement, their own greatness; when you open your heart on every distress and to all the unhappy — the sick, the handicapped, the homeless, the imprisoned, the malnourished, the exploited, the unlucky, the unloved and the joyless; when you work to help them or, even better, to teach them to be the artisans of their own success; when you build bridges, begin a dialogue, weave bonds of love between classes, peoples, nations and races for better understanding and mutual trust — the only conditions of a true peace which no pact, no treaty, no strike-force or deterrent can assure. The citizen of the kingdom of God is the "universal brother."

Who then will go recount to them the parable told by Jesus about the man who was attacked, robbed and left lying in his own blood on Jericho road? Two people of his own race and country — a priest and a religious worker — passed by him on the road; but whether through lack of concern, fear, or a desire not to be bothered, they pretended not to see him and went their own ways. It took a Samaritan (that is, a foreigner and a religious heretic from whom would usually be expected nothing but hate for a Jew in such a condition, with the thought "it serves him right!")—a Samaritan

The parable of the "Good Samaritan" is found in chapter 10 of Luke's Gospel.

who, moved with compassion, came to his rescue, bound his wounds, carried him on his mount to the nearest inn, paid the bill in advance and promised to check up on his progress on his return trip.

This story serves to make clear that one's neighbor is every man, no matter who he might be, whatever class, race, people or nation he might belong to, as long as he stands in need of love and a helping hand.

Moreover, every citizen of the kingdom of God knows that there is no limit to this love for others: "Love even your enemies," said Jesus, "do good to those who hate you. Be like God your Father... Look! He makes his sun rise, he sends his rain just as much for wrongdoers as for good people... ."

***

...Or to those who see in trickery and lies values both popular and necessary because "the end justifies the means." And who declare that life is successful when you don't burden yourself with scruples; when you have understood that faithfulness to your husband or wife, fidelity in treaties and alliances, and honesty in contracts or in business is simply naïve or stupid; when you realize that money and sexual passion rule the world, that no one is disinterested and that devotion and heroism are ultimately only foolishness; when you are able to "play the game," even if that means you play the role of a devout man... .

Who then will go proclaim to these people, echoing the voice of Christ, this turn-around of values: that on the contrary, your life is successful when you have a loyal heart, free from all duplicity and compromise; when you stay bound to the Truth and Justice, whatever the cost; when you observe this golden rule given by Jesus: "Say yes if your answer is yes; no, if it's no; anything more would be the work of the evil one" — and this other rule: "Do towards others what you would have them do towards you"; when you look at your neighbor with a kindly eye, more inclined to see the good that is in him than the evil; when you do not suspect others without proof, but trust them and give them the benefit of the doubt, even if you get no recognition out of it or suffer some hurt... .

Everything rests on the same law of love of the kingdom: "To love others as God has loved me." For everyone should remember how God has loved him with an obstinate love, in spite of his backsliding and forgetfulness. God himself knows what is in man, what risks he runs with his freedom; and God is full of mercy and forgiveness.

REFLECTIONS

**What Do You See In The Lives Of Individuals And Of Nations?
An Assortment Of Achievements Which Do Honor To Humanity...
But Also Stumbling-Blocks, Wars, And Ruins Which Carry Man To Despair.**

Friend and reader, you are no longer a child. You have joined mankind's long march, and the spectacle of human society unfolds before your eyes.
Yet what do you see?

In your own life and the lives of those surrounding you each day, next to real achievements in art, work, technology, the family, and the city; following on periods brightened by great gestures of generosity and noble feelings, there are sometimes — even often — zones of shadow, times of eclipse and heavy fog. You feel arising from the hearts of selfish men their tinny calculations, sordid self-interest, harmful intentions, bitter jealousies, terrible appetites for pleasure and domination.

Everyone more or less sacrifices to one or another of the many modern idols: promotion, the bank account, styles, sports, games, stardom, fancy dogs, horseracing, souped-up cars, the vacation home, the quiet and unbothered retreat. All these things can be good in themselves and are hardly damnable, but they become real idols when you give them your whole life, when you see no further than the horizon, when you become practically their slave.

What is true of individual persons is also true of the peoples whose history you study and who now move the surface of the earth.

Alongside brilliant civilizations which produce a galaxy of wise men and thinkers, philosophers and artists, writers and engineers; who build palaces and temples, libraries, universities and theatres, hospitals and clinics, factories and laboratories, highways and stadiums; who accumulate technical products of every kind, like SST's, color televisions, radars, moon modules and planetary landers; who defend the Rights of the Human Person, the rights of individuals and peoples to live as they wish; who take care to effectively help the less-developed nations... .

Alongside all these achievements, splendors and marvels, men participate in bloody revolutions, repressive dictatorships and murderous wars; people live in fear of atomic weapons, of airships with engines of total destruction, of submarines likewise armed roaming the ocean floors, of launch platforms ready to speed their loads of universal death. Citizens are shocked at the thought that in every minute which passes the nations of the world spend on armaments enough money to allow all the developing peoples to master their own development, if only they could be underwritten in their efforts for a period of ten years. We see whole populations made nationless and sent wandering around the world; concentration and extermination camps, economic structures and agreements which starve entire continents.

Every people builds its idols in its own image, and

it's always in order to render homage to Power, Money, Race, etc. No matter what names the idols go by — Nuclear Deterrent, the Free Market, Apartheid or Segregation, the Party Line — they all demand human sacrifice.

As you see, this is pretty far from the reign of God!

And You Come To Grips With A Difficult Task: To Plant The Seed Of The Gospel In The Minds Of Your Contemporaries And In The Structures Of Your Society.

You have surely met people around you who find the law of the reign of God such as it is written in the Gospel rather disturbing. If you have to take literally expressions like "be poor in spirit," "love your neighbor like yourself," "forgive your enemies," "remain faithful to your wife even in your thoughts," they say life would be impossible. It's all beautiful in theory, they argue, but it's not realizable in practice, at least in the real world. You can't take the gospel just as it's written... .

This is where you can measure how much the spirit of the earthly kingdom has contaminated even the best of men and how difficult it is to be an authentic citizen of the kingdom of God.

And yet it is necessary to carry the message of Christ to each person in his daily life and to society as it directs the movement of the world.

To the businessman, the industrialist, the physician, the lawyer, the shopkeeper preoccupied with how to make his fortune as quickly as possible, it must be said that the "law of love" asks him to consider his profession or career first of all as a service to others helping them to make something of their lives, and then as one means among others of giving a meaning to his own life and of living honestly.

To the businessman preoccupied with the profit and development of his factory, his farm business, his quarterly dividends, his success on the stock market, it must be said that the law of love asks him to be concerned in a primary way with the life of his workers, with their salaries, with dignity and health on the job; without forgetting the participation of his laborers and employees in the administration of the enterprise, for they are not merely machines, robots, or simple numbers on a time card.

To the employee obsessed with a fatter paycheck, scrambling after more and more overtime hours to the detriment of new workers who could be hired to do the extra work, who dreams of nothing beyond a secure and carefree existence where he can relax and laugh at the situation of the world and the advancement of his working brothers — to him it must be said that the law of love requires him to become concerned with the management of his factory, with decent labor legislation, with the defense and advancement of his fellow workers through union organizing or other collective endeavors.

To the writer, the journalist who makes a travesty of truth to serve a particular political interest, who aims at the base instincts of his readers in leading them to the garbage heap of gossip about the successive affairs and divorces of today's stars and starlets, and who exposes and orchestrates the latest reverberating scandal simply to sell more copy — to him it must be said that the law of love requires him to give the most exact information possible on facts and events, to put forth an objective, reserved, and lucid judgement in order to avoid exciting partisan hatreds, to cheapen no one with his writing, and to respect the intelligence and integrity of his readers.

To the husband or wife who gets a divorce and recreates his or her life once all the love is gone, to the mother who abandons her children because of some birth defect, to the woman who offers her body to the whims of men because she is forced to for money or for the satisfaction of her own sensual desires — to these people it must be said that the law of love requires them to love others — especially in marriage — as God has loved us; that is to say faithfully, with stubbornness, and in spite of our faults, our slips; to love one's wife not for the only satisfaction one finds there, but for her own sake; to love one's children, not selfishly because one sees oneself in them, but generously so that they can make of their lives the masterpiece that God dreamed they could become.

This list could be continued, but we still must move from the level of individuals to that of nations and peoples.

To the nation preoccupied solely with its economic development, the production of its agriculture and industry, its standard of living, the protection of its markets, ready to burn or destroy its surplus commodities, it must be said that the law of charity asks it to provide financial help, engineers, technicians, physicians, and professors to developing countries which are experiencing hunger, sickness, and infant death, and whose slum-dwellers must satisfy themselves with living off the food wasted or thrown in the garbage by the opulent cities.

To the state which bases its security and its strength solely on force and violence, trusting only to the destructive potential of its engines of war, it must be said that the law of charity wants all men to respect and to love one another as brothers, and that it asks the state to establish a dialogue of peace beyond its borders, to participate in international assemblies, to loyally allow controls on its territory and to halt the armaments race.

To the people which arrogates to itself the pretension of lording it over other peoples, under the pretext of cultural, technical, historical, or racial superiority; which crushes people with massacres and torture and psychological indoctrination; which depends on an all-powerful police state, lies, and persecution — to this people it must be said that the law of charity wants all peoples to accept one another as different and complementary, and that it asks a people to help other nations to grow and to realize their vocation in the history of humanity according to the genius proper to its race, to help cultural exchange succeed, and to respect the freedom of opinion and of religion.

To this humanity of the twentieth century which is developing at a breathtaking pace and which will soon have fantastic knowledge, riches and power, the "law of love of the reign of God" must more than ever be proclaimed. For if our atomic age is not immersed in this

law, humanity runs the greatest risks of self-destruction and the loss of both its body and spirit. But if this atomic age allows this immersion to take place, then we can look forward to the glorious achievement of the plan of God and the entry of humanity into the life of God.

Friend and reader, you are already convinced of this. And it could be that you will one day hear in the depths of your heart a call to be this "echoing voice" of the Christ who went through the villages and countrysides of Palestine proclaiming the law of love.

chapter five

Fishers of Men

>For a worldwide proclamation of the "law of love," for a renewal, a rebirth of humankind, Jesus invites the fishermen from Galilee — and many others after them — to become "fishers of men."

Andrew, Simon-Peter, James, John, Phillip, Bartholomew-Nathaniel — all these fishermen from the Sea of Galilee and some others besides became the faithful companions of Jesus. They expected to proclaim this new conception of existence, this reversal of the scale of values commonly accepted in a world of sin, this replacement of the "law of the jungle" with the "law of love."

But the question remained: who would traverse the wide universe and all its centuries to carry the message of the kingdom of God to men? And who would help these men to transform their innermost selves, to "change their hearts," so to speak?

Jesus once told Nicodemus, a man very much in the public eye but a seeker after perfection nonetheless, who had come to find him during the night to avoid gossip, "to enter the reign of God there is an indispensable condition to fulfill: you must be born again."

Nicodemus reacted with shock: "How is that possible? Reborn? Me, at my age? I can't see myself returning to my mother's womb to be born a second time!"

Jesus explained to him: "This rebirth is absolutely necessary; it is done through water and the Holy Spirit" (this was an allusion to the baptism he would later ask to be given in his name). "Look, what is born of the body is 'flesh'; what is born of the Holy Spirit is 'spirit.'"

By this he meant that since sin overcame the first human couple, man had lost one of his dimensions, the highest, the one which had crowned all the others: the divine. Once sin had been committed, man found himself in his simple natural state: man, period. That's what was meant by the words "what is born of the body is flesh." This was the only life which parents could communicate to their children. But as for a way to God, a life in friendship with him, these children were nonexistent or "stillborn."

So if God in his great goodness really wants to pardon the human race and give it once again this divine dimension, he himself has to communicate a new life to men. Thus we can rightly speak of a new birth. This is what Jesus meant with the words "what is born of the Spirit of God is spirit." In this way God's original plan is reestablished; and it is exactly this tremendous newness which Christ brought.

This account is taken from chapter 3 of John's Gospel.

But this change cannot be seen from the outside. And that's why Nicodemus was confused. Of course the action of God within man's heart is invisible; but it's still real. It could be guessed at, perhaps; for the new man of the reign of God will have a different mentality, a different way of judging things and of behaving. Within him, the "spiritual man" sweeps away the "fleshly man"; within him, the "law of love" replaces the "selfish law of the jungle" written in his flesh. The transformation is made in the depths of his being.

Nicodemus should have remembered the teachings of the prophets as well as the beautiful prayer found in the book of the Psalms attributed to David after his sin of adultery: "O God, create within me a pure heart, a new spirit."

The words of Psalm 50, the "Miserere."

He was already talking about a new creature even then. People had been waiting for centuries for a renewal of the human race.

Nicodemus, the evening visitor, went back a dreamer. But this conversation had really struck him. He would be found near Christ at a more tragic hour.

*In The Boat With A Man Who Could Master
The Powers Of Evil As He Calmed The Waves Loosed
By The Storm.*

So it was necessary not only to go carry the news of the reign of God, of this new conception of reality, but also to renew men within their depths in bringing them to know the evil and sin which threaten to bog them down, to capsize them.

Simon-Peter, Andrew, James, John and the other fishermen from the Sea of Galilee were better prepared than the rest to understand. For although the mentality of their people and their time grasped the symbol of running water, river water, as a sign of purification, life, and fruitfulness, the sea with its deeps, its monsters and its storms was felt to be the receptacle for evil forces and symbolized rebellion against God, evil and sin. A large part of their life was spent in struggling with the unfettered elements, out on the gaping waters always ready to plunge them into the abyss when a squall, quick and unexpected, would rage on this inland sea ringed by steep hills.

They could remember a notable crossing they made one day aith Jesus on board. Out on the open water a real storm let loose, stirring up enormous waves.

Jesus, tired from a long day of walking and preaching, was stretched out in the back of the boat, his head on a pile of ropes, sleeping soundly.

Yet the storm raged and the boat, pitifully small beneath the crests of the foaming waves, began to sink under the weight of the water which filled it little by little. In spite of all their work the fishermen saw that the situation was getting worse and that the evil forces, more ferocious than ever, would win out this time, swallowing them up without a trace.

Jesus was still sleeping, and such nonchalance toward danger was irritating. But, understanding that only a superhuman power could get them out of this, the fishermen pleaded with Jesus to rouse himself from his sleep: "Master, it's all over! We're going down! Ah, save us!"

With this cry of distress Jesus awoke and responded simply: "How could you be afraid? While I'm with you! How little trust you have."

Then, in the middle of these crippled men, hair all tangled, clothes sticking to their bodies, faces dripping, legs splashing in the water, and arms scrambling at the oars and ropes, Jesus rose up.

What boldness to stand up like that, facing the storm like a ship's sail, in danger of being swept away by the waves! But no —

This account is found in the disciple Mark's Gospel in chapter 4, as well as in the Gospels of Luke and Matthew.

Jesus started to threaten the wind, he scolded the storm, like the times he commanded the demons and the forces of evil: "Silence! Be quiet!" And he ordered the raging sea, "Be still!"

Just like that, as if tamed and dominated by a superior strength, the wind dropped and the waves subsided. Nothing more was heard but the quiet splash of a fishing boat sailing on a calm sea.

Simon-Peter, Andrew, James, John and the others stared at one another. The same question was on all their lips: "Who is he then? that the sea and the winds obey him like that!"

***

One other time the fishermen from the sea of Galilee understood that Jesus had absolute power over the forces of sin and evil, both symbolized in their eyes by the raging sea and the storm.

It was night. The wind was violent, the sea terribly agitated. They were rowing with difficulty. They were alone in the boat, Jesus having remained behind on the shore.

It could have been three in the morning when they spotted a human shape moving towards them, seeming to walk on the waves. They all thought it was a ghost and were ready to panic.

And the apparition began to speak. They recognized Jesus' voice: "It's me! Calm down! Don't be afraid!"

And it really was Jesus walking to meet them over the water, to their great disbelief. In the same way he had mastered the storm and calmed the sea, that night he showed them that he had the forces of evil under his feet — as he walked over the foaming waves and across the storm.

Simon-Peter understood. But couldn't Jesus give him a little of this divine power which overcame the forces of evil? After all, he was his friend...

This account is in Matthew's Gospel, chapter 14 (verses 22 to 32).

"Lord," he shouted, "if it's really you, order me to do what you're doing and come to you walking on the water as well!"

"But sure! Come on!"

And so Peter climbed over the side of the boat and began to walk on the water toward Jesus. He was so proud to tread underfoot this stormy and deadly water which had so often shown itself anxious to swallow him up... .

But he knew very well that he couldn't do it by himself alone. He needed Jesus, by whose power he was thus able to dominate the sea. But what if Jesus were to turn his attention elsewhere, not watching him advance toward him; wouldn't he be in danger of sinking?

At that moment, for as little as he had given in to the thought that Jesus would leave him to himself, Peter began to sink into the sea! "Lord, save me!"

Jesus put forth his hand and Peter clutched at him.

"Man of little faith! How little trust you have. Why did you doubt?"

Soon they were all back in the boat. The wind suddenly ceased.

"Now we have to recognize," they told him, "that you are endowed with a divine power."

"Go Out To The Deeps And Throw Your Nets!" – Fantastic Catches Are Waiting For You.

So this divine power to dominate the forces of sin and evil was Jesus' to pass on.

"Go to the ends of the earth," he would one day tell his companions, "teaching what I have told you, and baptize... I will be with you until the end of time." Which was to say: go everywhere to proclaim the "law of love" of the reign of God, this new conception of reality and the future of the universe; build the new creation; lead men out of the storms of evil and the deep currents of pride, selfishness, inhumanity, jealousy and hate which drown them in their raging waves; and baptize them for a new birth, a new life in the divine dimension, for a life of friendship with God and universal fraternity among men.

<small>This sending-forth of the apostles is in Matthew's Gospel, chapter 28 (verses 16 to 20).</small>

But before this final sending forth, Simon-Peter, Andrew, James and John had to hear the decisive call of Jesus to follow him.

They had to hear this call in the context of their very ordinary fisherman's life, but during one of those presences of the Lord at their side which would give a sign that could not be mistaken.

<small>This account is found in Luke's Gospel, chapter 5.</small>

On that day Jesus found them on the shore of the great lake, busy mending and washing their nets. He got into Peter's boat and asked him to put out from shore a little in order to better speak to the crowd which had come to hear him. Later, after speaking, he told Peter, "Go and cast your nets for the catch." Peter responded, "What for? We worked hard all night and caught nothing." But since Jesus insisted, Peter went ahead: "Since you have asked me, I'll go cast the net."

When he began to haul in his net, Peter was amazed at the catch. The net was so heavy and held such a beautiful catch that it started to tear in places. He had to call out to James and John in another boat to come help him. The two boats were soon so full they almost capsized.

Then Peter started to realize that something significant had just happened. He threw himself at Jesus' feet, saying: "Don't stay around me. I'm nothing but a poor man with a sinful heart."

"Don't worry, Peter," said Jesus with a smile. "From now on you'll catch not fish, but men!" And stepping onto shore, he told the four friends, "Get ready! Come with me! I will make you fishers of men."

That day they left their boats and their nets for good; and they followed him never to leave his side.

REFLECTIONS

Dear reader, it's better at this point to keep silent and stand back rather than to get into a long discussion.

I'm not going to tell you how and when God will call you to become a "fisher of men," or if he's really calling you. Competent counselors and advisors will help you discern the signs of a real "vocation." But you can be sure that the call heard by the fishermen of Galilee echoes each day in thousands of hearts around the world.

As you finish the first part of this book, remember that it is in opening your understanding to the widest horizons of mankind, in giving yourself generously and ardently to the most noble and neglected causes, in involving yourself resolutely in the struggles of this age so that the law of love of the reign of God can impregnate the minds of men and all the structures of society — yes, it is in all of this that you are best preparing yourself to hear the possible call of the Lord.

"Go forth!" Jesus said to Peter. Forth to the open sea where the wildest storms blow — but where the best catches are taken.

PART TWO

chapter one

Renewal for All

They followed Him enthusiastically, this man with the divine power to renew the world and change men's hearts.

With great enthusiasm the Galilean fishermen — Peter, Andrew, James and John — left their fishing boats, their nets, and their fellow workers to follow Jesus.

Others left even better jobs; like Matthew, the publican at Capharnum alongside the lake. He was an educated and important figure who had, moreover, made something of a compromise with the taxing power of the occupation forces. The publicans were for the most part seen as thieves and exploiters of their people's misery, and rightly so. But they also had some influence and could be useful at times.

Matthew, also called Levi, had met Jesus several times. And he too had been won over, just like the fishermen who often passed by his booth.

One day Jesus beckoned to Matthew: "You come too!" Matthew didn't give him the time to repeat himself. He left behind his account books, his money box, his good job, his career — everything; so happy was he to have gained the trust and friendship of Jesus. Where would he sleep? Under the stars, no doubt. Where would he eat? On the road, from handouts. But nothing worried him; he was beginning a great adventure.

This account is found in the Gospels of Luke (chapter 5) and Matthew (chapter 9).

Matthew was so happy to have freed himself from his burdensome and all too comfortable past that he wanted to celebrate the burial of his publican life with his friends. So he organized a copious banquet, something which scandalized all Capharnum.

***

There were about a dozen loyal friends and companions now following Jesus. And things were really happening!

They understood this not only in proclaiming the new life of the children of the reign of God, but they saw it as well in the astonishing proofs of this revitalization of humanity. Since what goes on in the innermost of men's hearts is not always visible and evident, Jesus proved his divine power to recreate and renew both persons and peoples by healing the sick.

They understood this well one day when Jesus was once again in this city of Capharnum. The crowd had overrun a house where Jesus had gone to receive them, and those who could not get in filled the adjacent streets. Four men came along carrying a paralyzed man on a stretcher. They were trying to clear themselves a path through the crowd to set their friend in full view at Jesus' feet. Giving up all hope of ever entering the house this way, they had the idea of climbing up onto the roof and making a hole between the beams in order to lower the paraletic on his mattress with strong ropes (we should point out that roofs in this country were often made of a kind of adobe spread out on cane supports).

This account is found in chapter 2 of Mark's Gospel and chapter 5 of Luke's Gospel.

Meanwhile, down below in the house, everyone began to wonder what was going on above; men threw up their arms to protect themselves from the bigger chunks of caked earth that fell on the gathering. What gall these men had! True, they were doing it for the sick man, but even so! Jesus, seeing the man land at his feet, admired their trust. The paralytic said nothing; but his begging stare said enough. Yet, even so, Jesus read in his heart that his illness was only the symbol of a much more serious paralysis. This man undoubtedly regretted his bad life; he really wanted to leave it behind him, but he believed that he was unable to "stand up" and begin a new way of living.

"Believe me, my son," Jesus said to the sick man, "I forgive you your sins."

And to those standing by who could've been astonished, even scandalized, by such boldness he said:

"Why are you thinking such evil thoughts of me within you? What do you think is harder to say to this man: 'your sins are forgiven!? Or 'stand up and walk'?"

They prudently kept silent. In fact both alternatives were difficult, one thing no more than the other, for they both called upon the power of God. But wait! One of the two could be verified; if it really happened, it would be proof that the other was likewise true: namely, that the Christ had the divine power to transform a soul into wholeness, to purify it absolutely of evil, to start it from new once again.

"So," Jesus continued, "I will show you that I really have the power to forgive sins." He turned toward the paralytic and said, "Stand up! Take your mat and go home." Immediately the sick man stood up before the amazed stares of those around; he took his mat and left, proclaiming all the while the goodness and the power of God.

***

Jesus' companions often saw this kind of unexpected and extraordinary healing take place before their eyes. Blind, lame, deaf, lepers — all were cured of their afflictions. A lot of people at that time mistakenly saw in certain kinds of nervous diseases and the like a kind of demonic possession at work. Since the one possessed was like a living image of the grasp of sin on the human heart, Jesus never missed the chance, every time it presented itself, to send such people away completely cured. He did so in order to make clear that his mission was to truly liberate humankind from evil.

All told, these healings of the blind, the deaf, the paralyzed, lepers, and men possessed by demons were not only proofs of the power and goodness of the Christ, Jesus, but were also signs that the reign of God was at hand. Men blinded by their errors, deaf to the voice of God, speechless to respond to it, paralyzed in their movement toward the good, stricken in their deepest selves with this leprosy of a habitual evil which rots and festers, possessed by a real spirit to do wrong—in short, numbed or shut off from divine

life, these people came to know a renewal in their innermost being, in going through a kind of new birth.

Jesus often said that to enter into the reign of God you had to be born again, but born this time to a better life of friendship with God. But how could you have proof for such a thing? What was needed was power over life and death.

Just so, the companions of Jesus would see him engaged many times in the course of their wanderings in a struggle with death — and triumphing every time.

While passing through the small village of Naim in Galilee one day they came upon a sad funeral procession. A young man, the only son of a poor widow, was being carried to the cemetery. The whole countryside was there to witness to their sympathy for the sad mother. Filled with grief, she was following her son's body to its final resting place, walking behind his litter.

This account is found in Luke's Gospel, chapter 7.

Jesus was moved to pity at the sight of the poor mother. He stopped her as she passed by and told her, "Don't weep!" He took a step and put his hand on the litter. The porters stopped. Then, with irresistible authority and great calm, he said simply: "Stand up, young man! I want you to." And behold, the boy rose up, sat on the litter, and began speaking. With a gesture full of love and a gentle smile, Jesus gave the child to his mother. You can imagine the amazement and enthusiasm of the people of Naim.

The companions would be present at a triumph over death even more spectacular because the dead man was already in the tomb for several days, the crowd was even bigger, and the whole business took place before the gates of Jerusalem, the capital. Jesus ordered the tomb opened and called in: "Lazarus, come out!" The dead man had been enshrouded, and they had to unwrap all his bandages and his shroud saturated with different oils so he could walk.

This account is found in John's Gospel, chapter 11.

The account of the procession with the palms is found in the four Gospels: Luke, chapter 19; Mark, chapter 11; Matthew, chapter 21; John, chapter 12.

The crowd was not put off. They recognized in Jesus the greatest conqueror of all time: someone who, in contrast to all the great warlords whose triumphs were but spilt blood and battlefields littered with bodies, had won a victory over death itself. Delirious with joy, the people of Jerusalem offered him a grand ovation across the breadth of the city, saluting him with palm fronds, branches from an always-green tree which was a symbol of a life which knew no death, and better suited to Christ than to ephemeral conquerors from the combat of war or from sporting games in the Olympic coliseums.

chapter two

Temptations of the Kingdom

The temptation to bring the Kingdom through prestigious human means without knowing suffering and sacrifice.

Peter, John, James, Andrew, Matthew, Bartholomew, Thomas, Judas, and the others, having become the loyal companions of Jesus, all had the opportunity to think that the installation of the kingdom of God would result from the use of prestigious means put at their disposal by Jesus who was seen as a kind of dispenser of divine power.

Several times they had been sent on missions two by two into villages where Jesus was going to pass, in order to make a first announcement of the reign of God. And they had received the power, in his name, to begin this transformation of men's hearts. They saw proof of this in the healings they worked on the sick and infirm, always in the name of Jesus. He even told them on their return, in response to their enthusiastic accounts, "It's true! I saw Satan falling from the sky like a thunderbolt!"

This account is found in Luke's Gospel, chapter 10.

And yet Jesus often warned them against what he considered the most dangerous of temptations. While they dreamed of glorious processions and triumphal entries, he spoke to them of files of condemned men carrying the instruments of their torture: "It is necessary," he said, "that everything predicted by the prophets about the Messiah be fulfilled. At Jerusalem he will be arrested and given over to his enemies. He will be mocked, tortured, condemned, and put to death on a cross. But on the third day he will rise again."

Some among his companions were able to recall the terms John the Baptist had borrowed from the prophet Isaiah to point out Jesus to them, the day of that first meeting with him on the banks of the Jordan: "See this man! This is the 'Lamb of God' who takes upon himself the sins of the world."

See this proclamation in the first chapter of John's Gospel (verse 29).

Six Hundred Years Earlier The Prophet Isaiah Saw A Vision Of The Servant Of God Offering Himself As A Hostage For Sinful Men And Giving Himself Up As An Atoning Victim.

In reality, the prophet Isaiah became the spokesman for a whole current of religious thinkers when he announced that the special person sent by God to the human race — the Messiah, as he was called — far from being a great conqueror or a powerful king like David or Solomon, would on the contrary be a "Servant" consecrated wholly to the service of God and men. The descendant of kings, he would take evil upon himself, bear the sin of men's darkest hearts and become the only really responsible man. Like a hostage suffers in the place of others, he would save humankind through the sacrifice of his life.

Isaiah, six centuries earlier, had painted a kind of portrait of the expiatory victim in these arresting and prophetic terms:

> The Servant of God; this is how we saw him:
> despised and rejected by men and women,
> a man of sadness, possessed by suffering,
> like the lepers before whom we cover our faces.
> Yet he bore our sufferings,
> he was struck down with our ills.
> And we thought him a beaten man
> struck down and humiliated by God.
> He was wounded for our sins,
> broken because of our crimes.
> The punishment which saves us is on him;
> and thanks to his wounds we are saved.
> All of us were like wandering sheep,
> each on his own way,
> and God weighed on him all our sins.
> Horribly treated, he humbled himself,
> he didn't open his mouth.
> Like a lamb led to slaughter,
> like a sheep dumb before his shearers.
> By force and judgment he was taken,
> and no one pleaded his cause.
> Truly, he was wiped out of the land of the living,
> for our sins he was stricken to his death.
> They put his tomb among the unholy,
> and at his death, he was with evil-doers,
> even though he never said anything wrong,
> nor put out any lie from his mouth.
> God was pleased to crush him,
> and he was run through.
> But if he offers his life in expiation,
> he will see his descendants, he will lengthen his days;
> and what is pleasing to God will be accomplished
>   by him.
> Through his sufferings, says the Lord,
> my Servant will justify many
> in taking upon himself their sins.
> He gave himself over to death
> and he was counted among sinners;
> even though he bore the sins of many
> and interceded for sinners.

This celebrated passage, one of the most dramatic and sublime in the whole bible, is found in chapter 53 of the Book of Isaiah.

There is an obvious similarity between the passion of Christ and this passage from the prophet which was written five centuries before the event.

Jesus' companions, to be sure, were familiar with this, the most famous text of the prophet Isaiah. But they preferred to be lulled by their dreams of prestige and power, their visions of triumph and vengence. The Messiah, the Christ

Jesus, they thought, would establish the reign of God over and against everyone by means of eloquent marvels, striking blows of signs, and smashing victories over their opponents.

One day as he heard Jesus speaking of going up into Jerusalem where he expected his arrest, condemnation, torture, and death, Peter tried to encourage him in what he imagined was a moment of discouragement: "But no! Look, such a thing could never happen."

Jesus whirled around, his eyes flashing anger: "Behind me, Satan! Tempter, get away! Feelings like those are not inspired by God. It's only man speaking in you."

And he clearly announced to his friends, "Whoever wants to follow me shouldn't be looking out for his own good. Instead, day by day, he should pick up his cross and follow me."

He was referring to the horrible file of men condemned to death whom the occupation troops would lead to their deathplace, forcing them to carry the heavy wooden crossbeam upon which they would die strapped to their shoulders. This was far from his friends' glorious processions and triumphant entries!

This account is found in chapter 16 of Matthew's Gospel (verses 21 to 23) as well as in chapter 8 of Mark's Gospel.

And Yet Jesus Himself Wanted To Experience The Temptation Of Building The Kingdom Of God With The Methods Of The Worldly Empires.

Jesus treated Peter like a "demon tempter" because his remarks reminded him of the trial he went through when he was preparing his mission.

After meeting John the Baptist on the banks of the Jordan, Jesus had retreated to the desert, fasting and doing penance for long weeks. (The desert, far from the world and its noise, is always the place for the supreme challenge and the decisive turning-point for religious persons.) Jesus, there as the champion of God's own cause, wanted to undergo the subtle temptation of forcing its triumph by prestigious human means, without undertaking the struggle between good and evil at the bottom of men's hearts. Couldn't he impose the reign of God through influence, force and power, suppressing all the evildoers on earth?

The demon tempter whispered to him: "If you are really the loved one of God, you should change these rocks, these pebbles, into loaves of bread." Which was in fact to say something like: "You should guarantee people the material well-being which they're striving for: comfort and pleasure. With money and technical know-how we can change these deserts into fertile oases. Then you'll be sure to succeed."

But God's work is not done this way. Even though it is important to transform the earth, it is still more necessary to act upon the heart of man. As long as this remains unchanged and unaltered, material abundance will only grow on man's spirit like a cancer. "Man does not only live by bread," Jesus responded to this temptation, "but by the word of God as well." What is important is to understand God's vision for man and to know what conforms to his plans for the world.

The demon tempter whispered again: "If you are the loved one of God, you should be able to accomplish marvelous deeds without fear of failure. Say, for instance, jumping from the highest tower of the temple to soar gracefully into the center of the stupefied crowd below." What an excellent way to seem to have come down from heaven itself, to take up the role of Messiah, to seduce the masses. Which was in fact to say something like: "Everybody loves stars, actors, winners, games and demonstrations of skill. Bread and circuses, that's what attracts crowds! It's a sure thing, a great way to be carried off in triumph!"

But God's work isn't done this way. For when someone gets the spotlight like this, it's his personal success which becomes important. He tries all sorts of fantastic and outrageous feats just to win the approval of an audience. But it's men's hearts which must be turned toward God; and this daily cult of idols only turns them further away. "You must not pressure God into action," Jesus responded to this temptation.

The demon tempter then threw out his ultimate assault. Conjuring up an image of all the riches of the world, the power of nations and the glory of thrones, he whispered this: "There's an easy way to succeed, even if yours is a spiritual mission. Team up with power; ally yourself with the leaders of nations and men in power. To do that, you'll have to get in their debt, worship them a little, flatter them.

The account of the temptations of Christ is found in chapter 4 of Luke's Gospel and chapter 4 of Matthew's Gospel.

The special literary style of this gospel passage will be noted. Christ made the temptations he wanted to undergo known to his apostles. But they are presented by the evangelists in a figurative style full of religious teaching.

You'll have to pay lip service to their way of seeing and governing the world, not criticizing their techniques of lies, tricks, force and violence." In short, it boils down to recognizing Satan and adoring him.

But God's work can't be done in such a way. And it's precisely in order to put an end to the domination of evil and sin that Jesus came on earth; in order to establish the reign of God in place of the "Prince of this World." And its method would thus be radically in opposition: "Get lost, Satan," Jesus concluded, "only God alone can be adored."

REFLECTIONS

Men And Women In The Church, Christians Faced With The Temptation To Do God's Work With Rich, Flashy Or Violent Means, Or By Compromises With Power.

Friend, your years of study and the first years of your adult life have already taught you enough to understand the seriousness of the reflections which follow.

The period we are living through and in which you find yourself called to give witness has known a strong and welcome drive for renewal in favor of an authentic Christianity freed from all compromise with the power of domination and privilege, stripped of all self-glory and triumphincy. And you are part of this movement of young people with hearts full of idealism and generosity, who are demanding of themselves a real honesty regarding their intentions and a true purity of means regarding their actions.

But we must remember that the best of men can always fall to the temptation to do God's work using all too human means, sometimes without even being aware of it, so persuaded are they of the need to do something to realize their goals. This happens because real situations are often difficult to judge and the tempter is well-practiced in sowing confusion in men's hearts.

When we study the history of the development of Christianity across centuries and continents, we are obliged to notice one thing: that some men and women of the church, some Christians, going along with the currents of opinion of their age, believed that the advancement of the kingdom of God in the hearts of men and the structures of society would be accomplished through the conversion of the leaders of nations, through the assumption of temporal power by the Pope and bishops, through the possession of territories (like the Papal States), through the amassing of prestige, glory, and the gold of great cathedrals, the pride of palaces and fortresses, through armed excursions against unbelievers or the "enemies of religion."

And often the reign of God wound up being contaminated by the spirit of the kingdoms of the earth; it also seemed to be "of this world." Once the religion of Christ became the religion of the state, the church was officially linked to government; and one registered one's opposition to state politics in rejecting religion, which in part explains the so-called "religious" wars. To fight to the death under the pretense of a disagreement about religious notions — how far removed from the gospel!

In other instances, the kingdom of God was imposed with the arrival of conquering armies, missionaries accompanying the soldiers. This, too, was fertile ground for confusion. The Christian religion was seen as part and parcel of the colonizer's civilization: their culture, their language, their art, their ritual. Resisting or detesting the invaders, these people of other races and other colors sometimes came to reject the God presented to them. What can be said of Christians who at one time organized the "slave trade," reducing black men to the status of slaves in contradiction to the most basic law of love?

In giving in to this temptation to bring about the reign of God through means all too human, through wealth or politics, the church of Jesus Christ was seen in many cases as more or less in league with temporal power; more or less linked to the rich classes, the "haves"; and more or less obliged to honor money and its possessors in its ceremonies and religious services — something wholly in contradiction to the gospel. Some men sincerely believed that the Christian religion would thus gain in prestige and that God's work would thus be

accomplished. But the people themselves, no longer recognizing the Christ of the gospels nor his fondness for the poorest of men, allowed themselves to be seduced by other doctrines which preached concern for the oppressed and unhappy, and left behind the church of the rich and privileged.

The story of the temptation of Christ in the desert will always remain appropriate. Power, prestige and wealth will always bring pressure to bear on the church, in order to take advantage of the influence it still has around the world. It is for the disciples of Christ to know how to defend themselves against it; and for you, friend, to keep it in mind, to the extent that you will be more decisively involved in the coming of his kingdom.

chapter three
The Least of the Servants

To make really clear that he came not to conquer, but to love to the end, Jesus stooped to the level of the least servants and washed the feet of his friends.

Jesus thus victoriously turned back these temptations. But some of his group let themselves be taken over. They believed God's work could be accomplished by grand means.

This was especially true of Judas. He followed Jesus and had become one of his close companions. He was convinced that Jesus was the Messiah; his preaching and his amazing deeds were proof enough of that. But he thought of him in terms of David, the conquering king, Solomon, the stately dictator and political trickster; and he looked forward to a bright future with a position as "Minister of Finances" in the new order that Jesus was founding.

But little by little he had to face up to things. Jesus passed up several opportunities of having himself named king and of seizing the leadership of a popular uprising. On the contrary, he was speaking of the sad end he was going to meet: arrest, condemnation, torture, death. He was heading for defeat, not victory.

Judas was an opportunist. And in spite of all the warnings, he refused to conceive of a Messiah according to the image of the "Suffering Servant" of which the prophet Isaiah spoke. He didn't resist the temptation of power and money. Evil gained ground in him. Realizing that all his dreams of glory were in danger, that he was mixed up in an adventure which would end badly, he made up his mind to cut his losses by going over to the side of Jesus' enemies and offering them the opportunity of taking him. He went to find them. He bargained the price of his treason: "What will you give me? — OK, it's done. I'll bring him to you." They struck a bargain: thirty pieces of silver. It was the price of a slave.

A slave... the least of all servants... that was it.

Judas's conspiracy is reported in chapter 26 of Matthew's Gospel and chapter 22 of Luke's.

The evening of the farewell meal arrived. Jesus knew he would be arrested that very night. He gathered his companions in a friend's house in Jerusalem. The solemn holy days of Passover were drawing near. It was — and still is — a sacred custom to observe at that time a ritual meal recalling the people's liberation from Egypt at the time of Moses. Jesus was serious; it could be seen that he was going to make some important declarations.

Jesus took his place at the table. At the same time a dispute arose among the companions about who was most worthy to occupy the seat of honor on such an occasion.

This episode during the Paschal meal is told in John's Gospel, chapter 13.

At that, Jesus got up from the table, took off his cloak and went to get a basin and a pitcher of water, hanging a towel from his belt. Then he poured water into the basin and went over to the couches where his friends were stretched out, feet on the floor in front of them. They watched him with blank faces.

And, like the least of servants, like a slave burdened with the most humiliating chore, he started washing his friends' feet, drying them with his towel. A more humbling gesture could not be imagined. Never would a good Jew have thus undertaken to wash the feet of his guests.

He came to Peter. The latter refused to have any part of it: "What? You, washing my feet!"

"Don't try to understand what I'm doing for now; I'll explain it to you later."

But Peter quickly pulled back his feet: "Oh no you don't! You're not washing my feet! Not on your life!"

"If you don't let me do this, you won't come into my sight again; we can only go different ways."

"Oh; well in that case, I change my mind. You can wash my hands and my head, too."

"It would be useless; that's not the point."

When he was finished, Jesus went back to his place. "Do you understand what I just did? Listen! Who is more worthy, he who is seated at the table, or he who serves the meal? The one sitting at the table, right? Well, among you I put myself in the place of the one who serves the table. You often call me 'Master' and 'Lord,' and you are right; I am that. But I, your Lord and Master, have washed your feet; you should do the same thing among yourselves."

He continued: "You know the kings and the leaders of nations lord over their subjects and like very much to be called the 'protectors of the people' or 'the fathers of the nation.' They are aware of their authority and power and they exercise it without pity. But as for you, do nothing of the kind. Let the eldest among you behave as the youngest, and let he who holds authority make himself the servant of the others. This will be the rule among you: he who wants to be the most dignified should make himself the slave of all. I give you my example; I have not come to be served but to serve and to give my life in ransom for a multitude of others."

He added, "My commandment is to love one another as I have loved you. That's how people will know you are my disciples. You are to love to the extreme limit; understand it well: there is no greater love than to give your life for those you love."

This gesture is repeated every year on Holy Thursday by the Pope in Rome, the bishops in their cathedrals and priests in their churches, as they wash the feet of young or poor people.

The words of Christ cited by the apostle John in his Gospel, chapter 15 (verses 12 and 13).

REFLECTIONS

Whoever Is Called To Follow Christ, To Dedicate Himself To The Service Of God And Man, Must Take To Heart The Words:
"Unless The Seed Die In The Earth, It Will Not Bear Fruit."

These words of Christ are a real challenge for whoever is called to follow him. This is surely no news to you. While trying to serve God and your fellow man, there can be no question of chasing after honors and titles, of looking out for yourself or your own interests. That would only show that you had understood nothing of the rule of love which covers everything in the kingdom of God and which can sometimes require the total gift of self even including death.

If some men and women in the history of the church have succumbed or even still succumb to the temptation to use the all too human means of force, power, and influence to quicken the coming of the kingdom, yet others — actually, quite a few — assumed and still assume the place of hidden servants. Examples abound. Great men and women from famous families with degrees and titles, who could have had brilliant careers, have made themselves poor and humble in monasteries, hospitals, schools, etc. Many more are willing to stay where they are, that is to say, to live and die as unknowns, in order to prepare neighborhoods, countries, or races to become more open to the message of Christ. Misunderstood pioneers to far-away lands, to "primitive" or under-developed peoples, to godless or hostile countries which imprison, deport, torture and put to death; apostles to concentration camps or "detention centers" who sacrifice their lives as hostages for others, and on and on. This is truly the application of Christ's words, "unless the seed die in the earth, it will not bear fruit."

If there was once a time when churchmen pursued career and advancement in a hierarchical structure, received secular honors and privileges as members of a special class of "clergy," and were well-regarded for their privileged possession of academic status and credentials, this time is long gone. God could one day call you to follow him, dear friend; even so, don't get wrapped up in illusions: you should rather expect to be ignored, unknown. For how many of the people you meet will see in you a holy person? The leader of a community of faithful? The bearer of the most sublime Truth ever to give meaning to life?. A spiritual father who transmits divine life? Not very many! Hardly a small fraction of mankind. But far from taking this lack of consideration with bitterness, you will feel it as a grace. For you will thus more surely join him who wanted to make himself "servant," the "hostage" of sinners. That's why you will make yourself humble and small, straining to become a "universal brother" with a heart full of love and friendship for all, especially the poor and sinners.

chapter four
For All Peoples, All Places, All Times

At the heart of his farewell meal, Jesus, "the servant," took the place of the ritual lamb, delivering himself "flesh and blood" as victim for the sins of humankind; and he charged his friends to repeat his action to bring men and women of all times and all places into his sacrifice.

The Passover meal was the most solemn meal of the whole year. A lamb immolated at the Temple was to be eaten, according to prescribed rules, in memory of the sacrifice offered by those ancestors the night of the first Passover: the night of their liberation from slavery in the time of Moses.

In the middle of the meal Jesus said to his companions, "I wanted with all my heart to eat this Passover with you before suffering. For I tell you, its meaning is going to be truly accomplished and realized."

And taking some bread (which was to be shaped like thin, flat cakes which were easily broken), he said the blessing ("I thank you Father, king of the universe, for giving us today the bread that we need"), and broke it into pieces, saying, "Take this and eat; this is my body given for you."

Then he took the large wine cup (probably made of bronze), which was sitting on the table full of wine; he said the blessing ("Blessed are you, Lord our God, for having created the fruit of the vine..."), and passed it around the table for everyone to drink, saying, "Take this and drink; this is my blood, the blood of the new contract between God and men, the blood spilled for you, for the multitude of men and women in remission of sins."

He added, "Do this in memory of me."

This scene is reported by Luke (chapter 22), Mark (chapter 14), and Matthew (chapter 26).

***

What did he mean by these words and gestures?

There was undoubtedly no lamb on the table that night. It was perhaps missing because the sacrificers had not yet slaughtered the thousands of lambs which the faithful were coming to offer at the Temple in Jerusalem before placing them on their tables for the Passover meal.

The night of the first Passover, in Egypt, the lamb's blood which marked and protected the houses of the Hebrews was linked to their liberation from slavery. But this night of the new Passover, it was a matter of a liberation even more profound: from the evil and sin which affected all humanity from the revolt of the very first human couple. The Christ, sent by God, a man like all the other men, a figure just as representative as Adam, took upon himself all the sin, all the evil which is within men's hearts. He bore it all, became responsible for it and, like a hostage who pays in place of others, freed them of it in the sacrifice of his life. He was the "Lamb of God" announced by the prophet Isaiah and presented to the world by John the Baptist, the Servant-slave taking away the sin of the world and reconciling humankind with God. His blood was the "vaccine" which killed the virus of sin and gave true life in the friendship of God to all who really wanted to share it.

At this sacred meal Jesus accepted his sacrifice ahead of time. In the depths of his heart he was already the victim. In the next days he was to suffer and to be immolated. He could already say, "Take this and eat, this is my body given for you... Take this and drink, this is my blood of the new alliance" (the real alliance, the true reconciliation of God with men). "Become one with me; enter the communion of this flesh, this blood" (flesh and blood was an expression of the day which meant the whole person, body and soul).

Jesus had added, "Do this in memory of me." It was necessary that the men and women of all times, all nations and all races could take part, could be in communion with his sacrifice, enter into its depths. They couldn't all be united with him at the precise moment of his bloody sacrifice; but they could all eat the bread become his flesh given up for them. Jesus asked his friends present with him around the table to repeat his gestures and his action in order to allow all men of all time and of every continent to situate themselves at this solemn instant — an instant become the "still point of a turning world" — when he gave himself as victim and when he convoked all humankind to participate, to commune at his sacrifice. He concentrated his companions in associating them at the very instant and very heart of his supreme sacrifice with his mission of reconciliation between humankind and God — a mission or ministry par excellence, a bridge of salvation thrown between heaven and earth. He charged them with the unprecedented mission to continue himself; to spread him, the God-man, throughout time and space, for the benefit of all men and women until the end of time.

This is how the eucharist should be truly understood.

***

His friends, eating the flesh and drinking the blood of the "Lamb of God" and hearing Jesus tell them, "Do this in memory of me" — did they understand fully? Perhaps not at the moment.

Yet they would have certainly recalled an event which happened some months earlier. It was the occasion of a great gathering of the people. The crowds, captivated by the words of Jesus, had followed him very far into the countryside. Once evening had come, Jesus didn't want to send them away without eating. But they were far from any settlement and didn't know what to do. The companion Phillip declared that no one had any supplies, except for a small boy who brought his cold meal: five cakes of bread and two fried fish. Jesus asked them to get the boy. And in his hands

This scene is reported in the Gospels of Mark (chapter 6), Luke (chapter 9), Matthew (chapter 14), and John (chapter 6).

as he divided them, the bread and fishes multiplied to infinity, to the point where the whole crowd could satisfy its hunger. And yet they, his faithful and close companions, had been charged by him with distributing the food. Amazed by this nourishing and never-finished bread which went through their hands in great profusion, they never suspected that they would later distribute around the world another bread both inexhaustible and the bearer of divine life.

The next day a large part of this crowd so marvelously nourished was in Capharnum, the nearest city, and heard Jesus make some really unsettling declarations, like: "You are looking for me because yesterday you ate all the bread you wanted. But there is a food much more important than the one you ate. For I am the real bread of life. And this bread is my flesh given up so that the world will have true life. You can always eat the other bread; but it does not keep you from death. Whoever eats my flesh will live forever."

No one understood how Jesus could give his flesh to eat.

What happened at the Passover table was the realization of this promise.

Words reported in the Gospel of the apostle John, chapter 6.

chapter five

The Sacrifice of the Cross

The next day, Jesus, the Lamb of God, innocent and mute before his judges, was tortured and immolated on the Cross. Through his sacrifice he opened to men the gates to paradise which their sin had closed.

The sacrifice of Christ was thus accepted and already consummated in the depths of his heart. The offering of the victim had been made; there was nothing left but to allow the immolation to proceed....

The "Suffering Servant" announced by the prophet Isaiah some five or six centuries earlier went to meet humiliation, injustice, torture and death. He would know humiliation: betrayed by one of his close companions, Judas; renounced by Peter to whom he had confided the responsibility and authority for the others; abandoned by all at the moment of his arrest, in spite of all their nice promises of fidelity; slapped around, treated like an idiot and an imposter, ridiculed — all this to make up for the conceit and prideful arrogance of men determined to play God.

He would know injustice: abandoning himself like a helpless lamb before judges reconciled to his destruction: Annais, Caiaphas, and the other religious leaders at

We refer the reader to the accounts of Christ's passion which hold an important place in the last chapters of each of the four Gospels.

Jerusalem; letting himself be condemned to the most infamous execution by an opportunist and delinquent Pilate; renouncing in a word his own defense in expiation for the wrong use of the freedom of men ranged against God.

He would know torture and cruelty: beaten, crowned with thorns, bearing his cross to Calvary, in a word making himself obedient up to the most shameful death in order to remove the sin of a humanity disobedient to its God.

And it was there, in the deepest humiliation, the most profound abandon between the hands of God, that sin, the demon, suffered the most radical defeat, with nothing left upon which to feed. Evil was going to be killed at its very root. So broke the dawn of the new life of friendship with God; thus humankind, freed of his slavery to evil and reconciled with God, could regain its access to divine life.

***

This reopening to God began on the cross itself, on

Calvary, in the most moving scene, in the most gripping human drama.

Along with Jesus they had crucified two other condemned men who were thieves; he thus found himself lifted above the earth on his cross between two criminals.

One of the two wrongdoers nailed to the cross, cursing his suffering and hurling his hatred on the crowd to come to feed on their agony, turned on Jesus for a moment: "Well, if you're the Christ, what are you waiting for? Free yourself and us with you!"

This episode is reported by Luke in chapter 23 of his Gospel (verses 39 to 43).

But the other was impressed by Jesus' attitude. And he undoubtedly was familiar with him; perhaps he had met him, been present for one of his miracles. He had heard people speaking of a new kingdom about to begin where life would be good, where men would no longer prey on other men, but would love one another like brothers; a kingdom which would start on earth but would endure after death in friendship with God. And then this sad man, having tried to lead a better life, fell back into his ways. Now it was all ending on a cross.

Yet the night was not utterly dark; a fire still burned within, a small spark in the ashes. He tried to silence his partner on the cross who was spewing forth insults on the other side: "Why don't you shut up! Don't you even fear God's judgment? You should, since you've been condemned as I have. For the two of us, it's just. But as for him, he's innocent; he never did anything wrong."

Anyone speaking on Jesus' behalf on Calvary had to be an outlaw. But this act of witness at this all-important moment unexpectedly made things much clearer for the thief; he began to feel that his life could still have a meaning, that he still had a chance, perhaps the best chance of his life: he was next to Jesus when it counted. He looked at him and asked him simply, "Jesus, remember me when you come back to begin your reign."

Jesus turned his head toward him and answered, "I promise you, this very night you will be with me in paradise."

REFLECTIONS

From The Supper And From Calvary, The Two End Points Of The One Sacrifice, Spring Forth Both The Church And The Priesthood

Before this cross stretched out on Calvary where Christ has died, we need to stop to reflect on where we find ourselves.

For it is here in a single sweep of this wide horizon that we can grasp the real meaning of church and priesthood.

Christ, the God-man, is often called the "second Adam" in the scriptures. This is to say that he is the prototype of a new humanity; a prototype that includes all men and women in its newness and remodelling, a prototype that allows all humankind to rediscover the divine element it once lost through the first Adam's fault.

We have all heard the modern technical term "prototype." It refers to a model, the first example of a new kind of thing, of a new "race" of machines. In a sense, it includes them all, it is them all, it is found in them all. If there has been an error or deliberate sabotage on the level of the prototype, then all the machines being built from that prototype will bear the same fault; this will prevent them from realizing the aims set by the engineer who designed the original model. A new prototype would be needed to correct the situation. This new model would be perfectly formed, and it would make possible the correction of all the faulty machines copied from the first prototype. Then they would be able to perform to expectations; they would be able to meet their original goal, and their existence would finally make sense. Just as the first prototype included all the machines, the second would also include them, would bear them within itself, would be in all of them. This is undoubtedly a really materialistic model of things, but it may help us to understand Christ's position.

Adam, as we call the first human person in the full sense of the words, was like the first prototype of humankind; he disfigured God's achievement within himself. Abusing his freedom, he considered himself great enough to play God; he wanted to create himself, all by himself; "you will be like gods," whispered the demon. But, turning in on himself, he fell back on his own tyranny and became the slave of evil and sin. A secret slavery, perhaps, and one in which he could find delight: thanks to his intelligence he was still the master of creation. He could be successful, organize the world and find happiness. But he was locked in his biological role of an intelligent animal. He lost his divine possibilities, lost his "Paradise", an image and symbol which expresses the intimacy of his life with God in the freedom of a child, like a son with his father.

Christ, the second prototype of humankind, came into the world and into history. He bore within himself God's forgiveness and the power to communicate to men the divine life which filled him. Man like other men and women, he took their sinful flesh. In solidarity with them he behaved as the responsible one, and entered into a decisive struggle to free his brothers and sisters.

To do so he assumed a role contrary to that of Adam the rebel. He accepted the whole of the human condition from the moment of his birth. He lived the life of an ordinary man, in a given time, in a specific country and specific village, with a definite style of life and a definite occupation. He was familiar with all human necessity: he ate, drank, slept like everyone else. Beyond that, he made himself a servant, the hostage designated to replace the guilty. He went to the extreme limit, the rockbottom of all dejection: betrayed, abandoned by all, whipped, tortured, he took on himself all the sins of the history of the world. And he completed the sacrifice of the "humiliated servant" to repair the damage done by the "leader of a rebellious race."

Evil, the demon, no longer had any hold, could act on nothing at all, and thus lost all its power. Sin was conquered. Suddenly the barrier which kept humankind from assuming its divine dimension was lifted: it could rediscover its forgotten intimacy with the Father because God had accepted the sacrifice of his "humiliated servant" and proved this in resurrecting him.

On Calvary Jesus reopened the way toward the Father when he told the criminal who regretted his evil past, "I promise you, this very night you will be with me in Paradise." So it was a man of really obvious guilt, a thief, who first reentered this path.

For this man united himself to Christ in his sacrifice; he agreed to let himself be torn away from the servitude to evil which bound up his heart. He set himself on the side of the new human prototype; he surrendered to God. He was "saved," he pursued his "salvation" — which is what Christianity is all about. Onto the old human nature inherited from the first prototype of man, it was necessary to graft Christ; as a barren tree receives the graft of a living and fruitful branch. So life is transformed, transfigured.

To be sure, it is something of a radical break, a

change of heart, a "conversion," to be united with Christ in his sacrifice. We might have to give up our secret slavery, like a grafted trunk gives up its own branches. We have to convert ourselves to a wholly new way of thinking, as we noticed in talking about the "reign of God"; and to do so we have to leave behind a way of living where we are satisfied with our selfishness, our interests, our quiet, our comfort, our lack of love for others, our habits of sin. And the price is nothing less than to be a disciple of the crucified. What's really wrong in the world is that this victory won by Christ can be canceled, rendered useless for one person or another. For man's freedom resists the love of Christ which presses on him. And God respects this freedom.

Continuing this work of salvation, bringing men and women of all times and all races to God in proclaiming his Christ, submerging them in the saving sacrifice forever being set before them ("Do this in memory of me," Jesus said), grafting Christ onto them in order to have them flourish with a new, divine life — in short, making them new persons on the model of Christ and thus sons and daughters of God — this is the essence of ministry in the church of Jesus Christ. And these are the reasons one becomes a priest.

Philosophers and scholars, scientists and technicians, sociologists and economists, politicians and labor leaders, artists of all kinds — the world needs people like these to reach its fulfillment. Christian writers and thinkers, authentic disciples of Christ in all fields and all social classes who put the law of love of the reign of God in their lives — the world also needs people like these to bear witness to Truth. These are all useful and necessary vocations, at once different and complementary.

But the priestly vocation is indispensible among all others, in order that Jesus Christ, the only bridge of salvation between heaven and earth, be made known and spread throughout the universe; and so that humanity, now given the new life it was meant to have from the first instant of creation, may find itself in God.

In The Bowels Of The Earth

At three in the afternoon, on the sabbath eve of Passover, Christ died on Calvary. After promising for that very night the "Paradise" of eternal friendship with God to one of the criminals at his side, his last words were a cry of confidence and abandonment: "Father, I put my spirit in your hands." And bowing his head, he let his heart shatter.

It is thus that the gigantic struggle of cosmic proportions that unfolded on Golgotha broke loose in the ultimate confrontation between the God-man and the demon, evil, and sin; broke loose like a spiritual tempest with repercussions in nature itself. The earth shook, boulders were split, and at the Temple a tornado which blew up from nowhere descended on the courtyard where thousands of lambs were being sacrificed. It ripped off the curtains of the sanctuary as if to make plain that there would no longer be any need for a Temple now that the single sacrifice of the true "Lamb of God" reconciling heaven and earth was finished.

To be sure that Jesus was really dead, a soldier from the execution squad pierced his heart with the iron point of his sword. And John, one of Jesus' close friends present at the final moment of Calvary, saw blood and water flow from the wound. He was to later understand that these twin streams were meant to purify and cleanse the world of its stain; and he could remember the words of the prophet who spoke of an unhoped-for salvation issuing from the suffering and the

This account is found in chapter 19 of John's Gospel (verses 31 to 47).

mysterious death of an only son: "And they will look upon the one they have pierced." (The prophet could not have put it any better, since for over 2,000 years people have turned again and again to the face of Christ dying on the cross.)

They finally took down the body of Christ and put it in a nearby tomb, all new and hewn in rock, and sealed it with a great rolling stone.

chapter six
The Risen Christ

Life and death met in a great struggle — Christ has risen from the dead. He gave his companions the mission and the power to communicate to mankind his divinizing energy and promised to be with them until the end of time.

The day after the Sabbath of Passover, some women went to the tomb carrying spices with which they would express their love and care for the man crucified on Calvary. How great their amazement to find the tomb wide open! They ran back and alerted Jesus' companions. Peter and John, running to the tomb, verified the women's story; and they were able to recall that Jesus predicted several times that he would be arrested, tortured and put to death, but that he would rise from the dead on the third day.

And that's how it happened. Mary Magdalene was first to see Jesus alive. On the road to Emmaus going out of Jerusalem, a couple of Jesus' disciples left utterly hopeless by his death on Calvary — and what a death: the death of an outlaw! — were joined by an unknown stranger. The latter questioned them on the reasons for their sadness, and took the trouble to explain to them how, according to the prophets, Jesus had to realize in his life the figure of the "suffering servant" and go through trials, torture and death before breaking forth in his triumph. He did this so well that in their own hearts the two disciples were ready once more to hope.

Soon they came into Emmaus and he made as if he were going to continue on the road. But they insisted that he stay with them. Together they sat down to table. Then he, with all the authority of the master of the house, took the bread, pronounced the blessing, broke it into pieces and gave it to his two companions. At that moment, in that sign, they recognized him. It was Jesus. But, as fast as he was recognized, Jesus was no longer there; he had disappeared. They looked at one another, questioned one another; but very quickly they realized: "It was really him! So he has really risen from the dead. Oh, we should have realized it earlier... He really had a way of giving us confidence when he spoke to us along the road. Our hearts were truly moved."

In no time they took to the Jerusalem road once again, going back to spread the good news. They no longer felt their weariness.

They found Jesus' companions reunited, and were greeted with these words: "Friends! Fantastic news! Jesus is risen. He has appeared to Peter."

"And to us too! Listen." And the two travelers from Emmaus told them what had happened on the road and how they recognized Jesus in the breaking of the bread.

These resurrection accounts are found in the Gospels of Luke (chapter 24), Mark (chapter 16), Matthew (chapter 28), and John (chapter 20).
The account of the "companions of Emmaus" is in chapter 24 of Luke's Gospel.

They were still talking about it when a voice not unfamiliar to them signaled a presence: "Peace be with you!" (This is an ancient form of greeting which expresses care for the other's well-being.) Jesus appeared among them.

And yet the doors were solidly shut; everyone was rather on edge, especially since the rumor started to spread that Jesus' tomb had been found empty. How did he get in? A mystery! They were all speechless, glued to their places, asking themselves if they weren't seeing a ghost before them.

"What's bothering you all? You don't seem too reassured to see me. Do you still doubt? But look at my hands, my feet. It's really me. Touch me; make sure for yourselves. A ghost doesn't have flesh or bones, and you can see that I have both."

But they still didn't dare to believe. They were afraid they would regret an instant of false joy later on if they mistook their deepest wishes for reality.

"Do you have anything to eat?" he asked them. They gave him a piece of toasted bread and some fish. Before their eyes he took fish and bread and ate. At last their remaining fears evaporated; they were sure they were not in a dream. It was really Jesus. They all bubbled over with joy.

Divine Force

Christ had gone on to a new state of life. A godly energy glorified and spiritualized his body from the moment the opaque barrier of sin he took upon himself disappeared in his sacrifice on Calvary. Jesus was no longer bound by the usual conditions of earthly life; he went beyond the barriers of time and space and moved body and soul into a new kind of existence.

But as the "prototype" of a new humankind, the first-born of all who had until then been dead to divine life, Jesus committed himself to communicating his godly energy to men and women of all times, places, and races who would unite themselves to him in his sacrifice and thus be reborn and resurrected with him to a new life.

And for that he charged his companions with a mission and transmitted his powers to them. His last command was thus: "Go, carry the good news of the reign of God to all the nations of the earth. Gather disciples, baptize them and teach them to observe all that I have taught you. I will be with you always, even until the end of the world."

***

He would thus always be acting in them and through them. He would always be there within them, present but unseen. Since his resurrection he had taught them to believe in his continuing presence; sometimes he was suddenly present among them talking, eating, walking with them, letting himself be touched — and unexpectedly he would show himself no longer. Like a good teacher, he wanted them to learn to act on their own, without expecting every initiative to come from him; in a word, he wanted them to be adult in their faith. He would trust them fully, for his part; he would sanction their decisions and make them his own. Through his presence within them, he would guard them from every fundamental error, even though he left to them the choice of means and all their human weaknesses.

<small>Luke's Gospel, chapter 10 (verse 16).</small>

Would they speak; would they teach? It would be Jesus speaking, Jesus teaching. He told them, "He who hears you, hears me; he who rejects you, rejects me."

<small>Mark's gospel, chapter 16 (verses 15 to 18).</small>

Would they baptize? Would they anoint the sick? It would be him baptizing, healing. He told them, "Go, baptize. Lay your hands on the sick."

<small>John's Gospel, chapter 20 (verses 21 to 23).</small>

Would they forgive sins? He would do the forgiving. He told them, "The sins you will forgive will be forgiven; the sins you don't forgive will remain a burden."

<small>Luke's Gospel, chapter 22 (verse 19).

First letter of Paul the apostle to the Christians at Corinth, chapter 11 (verses 24 and 25).</small>

Would they celebrate the Eucharist, repeating the actions and words of Jesus' farewell supper where he changed bread and wine into his body and blood? It would be him breaking the bread in their hands and speaking the sacred words through their lips. He had told them at that supreme moment, "Do this in memory of me."

<small>Matthew's Gospel, chapter 28 (verse 20).</small>

Would they lay their hands upon others to bestow a mission, a duty? It would be Jesus designating and consecrating others as new apostles. For he had said, "I will be with you until the end of time." The apostles thus needed to find their successors.

REFLECTIONS

**The Waters of Baptism
Whoever Christ Calls To Follow Him
Receives This Sublime Mission
To Revitalize Humankind In The Waters
Of Baptism.**

We saw in the first part of this book how Jesus gathered his companions and all the others to follow him, and sent them around the world to proclaim the reign of God and his law of love. Now in the second part

we have seen that they were also given the mission to "submerge" others in his death and resurrection, to free them from the evil of sin and give them a share in his godly energy and thus make them new creatures, raised to the royal dignity of sons and daughters of God.

And this is what the apostle Paul explained to the first Christians: "Through our baptism we were laid in the tomb with Christ in his death so that just as Christ rose from among the dead we in our turn will live a new life."

And this is why, in the first days of the Church, to mark this purifying and renewing "passage," baptism was administered in a great cistern full of water where those who were becoming Christians were plunged, immersed as if in a tomb. Going in on one side, they got

out on the other, as if crossing a river. Before entering the baptismal fountain, they left behind all their clothes to symbolize their stripping-off, their renunciation, of a former way of life. And as they emerged baptized according to the treasured formula, they dressed in new white clothes which they were to wear for eight days to symbolize their liberation from sin and the new glory which they wore on their hearts. Finally, they received a new flame which signified the new inner light of a Christian overcoming the shadows of sin, as well as the new divine life which shone from within them.

Thus, in asking others to be baptized in his name, Jesus made this symbol of purification a sacred sign which truly produced within men's hearts what it was supposed to signify: that man is freed of his sin; that God's forgiveness is assured him; that his person is radically renewed and completed. Although he remains a member of Adam's race, he is no longer bound simply to his biological role of an intelligent animal, but can rediscover the divine status which is his according to God's original plan. He is reborn in the divine life given him by Christ.

This life can well remain hidden and unnoticed; but it really exists. It is "eternal life," heaven already begun; the same as a seed is already the beginning of a real flower in all its future beauty.

The Pardon of Sinners
The Priest Also Receives The Divine Mission To Forgive In The Name Of Jesus Christ Anyone Who Falls Once More To The Evil Spirit And To Reintegrate Him Into The Family Of The Sons Of God.

The old man of sin still sleeps within the heart of the

baptized Christian, who is always free to make compromises with evil. And it is very difficult to strip oneself completely of the mentality of the kingdoms of earth which one inherits in being born into the world — and which sleeps in the dark depths of the heart with all its perversions and its selfish law of the jungle — in order to put on the "new man" of rightness and perfection. The evil and sin in the world saturate us and attack us from every direction. And in our own hearts there are always rationalizations which will give them an entry.

Luckily enough for humankind, God loves man with an obstinate love which follows him everywhere, no matter how far he wanders. God loves us like the father of a boy who lets himself be reconquered by the spirit of evil. The sinner loses his divine status, his rights as a citizen of the kingdom of God. But God waits for him always. He stands at the roadside, ready to welcome him, to give him the dignity of a son. The only thing necessary is for the errant boy to express a gesture of regret, to take the first step homeward. And he'll see God come out to meet him.

Those Jesus calls to follow him and to whom he has given his powers of forgiveness will remember the story of the "Prodigal Son." There Jesus compares God to a good father whose son left home demanding his share of the inheritance and went on to throw it all away in foolish fun and games — right up until the day when his pockets were empty and he found himself forced to clean a pigsty in order to have enough to live.

In his sad condition he started to think about the good times he had as a son under his father's roof: "My father's servants have as much bread as they want, while here I am dying of hunger. I can't keep this up; I'm leaving, I'm going back to my father. I'll tell him, 'Father, I've sinned against heaven and against you. I am not worthy to be called your son. Treat me like the lowest of your hired help.' "

This parable is found in chapter 15 of Luke's Gospel.

And so he was on the way home. He saw his father's roof. He dared not take one more step.... But who was that down there coming toward him?

His father had never reconciled himself to his son's going. He might be a drunkard and a fool, but he was still his son. Since he had left home, the father had been utterly sad and despondent. His heart wept. The unhappy child was still far from home when his father saw him on the road. You had to be a father to recognize from such a distance the rag-covered figure with no coat and no shoes as the ungrateful and independent son who had so proudly taken off several months earlier.

Touched with compassion before such misery, impelled by the goodness which overflowed his heart, there went the father, running to meet his son. He held him in his arms, and without giving him the time to say a word, embraced him warmly.

The prodigal then began his confession. He would have left his father's embrace in order to throw himself at his feet, but that was impossible. He sobbed the phrase he had learned by heart: "Father, I have sinned against heaven and against you. I am no longer worthy of being called your son." But the father would not permit his son to continue; and the son understood that to talk about assuming the position of a lowly servant to such a father would hurt him very much. There was nothing left but to weep in joy and recognition.

So there were the two of them walking together back toward the house. And it is likely that the first servants they met showed a crafty smile in seeing their master's son: "Well, look who's come home — and in what a state!" The father was not about to put up with anything of the kind: "What are you standing here for? Go get his best clothes and help him dress. Find him a ring (a family sign and a symbol of his rights as a member) and some shoes. And go round up the fatted calf; slaughter it. We're going to have a banquet to celebrate

the return of my son. Think about it! I took him for dead, and here he is come back to life; I thought he was lost forever, and here he is found."

***

The priest is the one who has received this mission to make known to the world the limitless goodness of God for man and to dispense forgiveness in his name with open hands. His, then, to live in contact with the greatest sinners — with Jesus' help and all the good sense necessary.

Christ gave an example: "Look at the prophet!" the Pharisees, the supposed "thinkers" of the time, said about him. "Look at him eating with the rabble from the cities and slums!" And thinking that they were insulting him and bringing down disgrace upon him they called him "the friend of the sinners and wrongdoers." Yet there's no better title to sum up the mission of Christ, who responded to them one day: "You don't go to get the doctor for the well, but for the sick. And know that I have not come to convert those who do good, but those who remain in sin." Another time, responding to the self-conceit and ill-will that these men held out to him and his following of poor people kept outside the society of that day, he hurled this ringing condemnation: "I give you my word: those thieving publicans and prostitutes will see the reign of God before you all!"

Mark's Gospel, chapter 2 (verses 15 to 17).

Matthew's Gospel, chapter 21 (verses 28 to 32).

In fact, the gospel tells us the story of a woman called Mary Magdelene, a prostitute who came to throw herself at Jesus' feet during the course of a dinner at the home of a pharisee named Simon. What was going on in the heart of this "easy woman"? She had heard Jesus and began to understand that there was a greater, more beautiful love. She decided to leave her life of sin to enter into the reign of God. And she was so happy no longer to be walking the streets selling her flesh to the whims of others that she wanted to thank the one who had pulled her out of her shame, who had resurrected her heart. So she did this in her own way, in a manner so unselfconscious that it shocked the others; she caressed his feet and bathed them with an expensive perfume.

This account is found in Luke's Gospel, chapter 7.

But she became troubled and began weeping; her tears ran onto Jesus' feet. Very quickly she undid her long hair and began drying the feet of her savior. There she stayed, head lowered, bewildered by her own boldness, feeling the weight of the diners' stares on her back.

For they were shocked, outraged, scandalized. And Jesus had to make the pharisee Simon, his host, understand all the difference between the easy and uncompromising way in which Simon had invited Jesus to his table, and the demonstration of true, spontaneous and unselfish love which characterized the sinner resolved to change her life. "Go," he told her, "your sins are forgiven."

The gospel also records the meeting between Jesus and the publican Zaccheus, a man like scum in his neighbors' eyes, due to his thievery and his collaboration with the Roman occupation. This untrusted functionary wanted to see Jesus, but only out of curiosity, for he considered himself incorrigible and doomed to divine wrath. Even if he wanted to change his life, he thought it was too late for that — or so he believed.

This account is found in Luke's Gospel, chapter 19.

Perched on top of a sycamore tree which probably rose over the street from his garden, he watched the crowd cheering Jesus as he crossed Jericho. And then there was Jesus, stopping only a few steps from his perch in the tree. He looked up in the branches where Zaccheus was hiding and shouted with a broad smile that lit up his face, "Zaccheus, come down quickly: I want to rest at your house today."

What? Could this be happening? Yet Zaccheus had heard correctly. And above all, he had felt Jesus' look penetrate into his heart. Undistracted by all the gibes which rose up to him from the street, he jumped down from his tree and ran breathlessly to his house. Later on in the day, he welcomed Jesus into his home. People in the city were scandalized. How on earth, among thousands of inhabitants, had Jesus chosen one of them? But Jesus, who reads the hearts of men, knew who needed his visit the most; he also knew whose heart was most open in spite of appearances.

And in fact it was a new Zaccheus who welcomed Jesus; for he had resolved to change his life and become a citizen of the kingdom of God. He was aware of all his faults. With Jesus present as a witness, he publicly declared, "Here is what I have decided: I am giving half of what I own to the poor; and whatever I have stolen I will repay four times over." Then Jesus told those who came with him to Zaccheus' house, "Today this family has received salvation. And this is really what my mission is: I have come to look for and save those who were lost."

***

So it is with the priest, who has been given this mission to forgive those who fall once again under the control of evil and to reintegrate them into the family of the sons of God; the priest is by vocation at the service of sinners. In the third part of this book we will see the requirements of such a life of service.

The priest is there to remind all prodigal children that they are always being followed by the obstinate love of a God who wants them to live, not die; and that there is no fault so great that forgiveness cannot be found — on the sole condition that we recognize our situation and take the first step back toward God. And even then, God's help is always there to support that first step.

In Christ's service he has learned that no man's situation is ever hopeless and that no life situation can stand in the way of the reign of God. He never recoils from being called, like Jesus, a "friend of sinners," from being concerned with people seen as worthless in others' eyes: delinquents, prisoners and ex-cons, drug addicts, the down-and-out. Those who refuse to see the worth of people like these often show that they have understood nothing about the law of love of the reign of God. Moreover, who among them can claim that he never weighed heavily upon the shoulders of the Good Shepherd — to use the image of the lost sheep which the shepherd brings back to the fold?

His whole life long the priest remembers that since he has been called to follow Christ, he is, like him, a mediator between sinful humankind and God; he is thus a hostage who bears responsibility for his guilty brothers and is unable to ignore his solidarity with them. Following Christ, he accepts the sins of men and women in order to liberate others.

Shepherd carrying a young ram on his shoulders.

For many centuries the image of Christ the "Good Shepherd" was more popular than the figure of "Christ crucified."

***

The Sacrifice of Calvary

On Over 200,000 Altars The World Around Priests Have The Responsibility Of Bringing Before The Men Of All Times And All Nations The Unique Sacrifice Of Calvary.

The first baptized Christians at the beginning of the Church gathered regularly to hear the companions of Jesus, the Apostles, speak about their master and his teaching. They formed one great family, loved one another as brothers and sisters, and put all their goods in common to care for the poorest among them. And they prayed together with one heart, especially when they gathered for the "breaking of the bread."

This term refers to the eucharistic rite, what we have come to call the "Mass."

In the evening, they gathered intimately in the house of one of their number. This assembly of the disciples of Christ — or "Christians" as they were soon to call themselves — began with a small meal, to which everyone brought one dish to share with the others. Then they set aside some bread and wine. One of the apostles present would repeat the words and gestures of Jesus at the end of his farewell supper. Taking the bread he would say, "This is my body..."; taking the cup of wine he would say, "This is my blood, the blood of the new covenant between God and men, blood spilled for you, for the multitude of men in the remission of sins." In doing so, the Apostle identified himself with Christ, took his place in order to obey the command, "Do this in memory of me." Then he would break the bread and distribute it to the united disciples. Afterwards he would pass around the cup of consecrated wine from person to person. Each one received "Communion"; that is to say, each person united himself to Jesus present among them under what still seemed to be bread and wine.

This was the only ritual innovation of the first Christians, but it was significant. Everything was expressed in this new rite: the church was the "sharing of the bread."

And so the eucharist is the central act of all Christian ritual. Why? Because it is the sacrifice of Calvary, the culmination of world history, being brought to men of all times and all nations.

When Christ said at his last supper, "This is my body given up for you" over the bread and "This is my blood spilled for you" over the wine, he was accepting his sacrifice at Calvary in advance. In the following days he would be immolated. But he wanted his companions to be able to unite themselves to his sacrifice, to be in communion with this "body given up" and this "blood poured out."

In asking them to repeat these words and gestures, it was as if Jesus wanted them to make this supreme instant stand still until the end of time; this instant during which he gave himself up as an offering for all humankind and invited all eras and all continents to unite themselves to his sacrifice: "Take this and eat..., take this all of you and drink.... ."

To obey this wish of Christ, the bishops as successors to the companions of Jesus and the priests who share their powers (and who number around 250,000 in the world today) celebrate the eucharist every day. We can only admire this marvellous invention of Christ which allows all men and women to be present with his companions at his farewell dinner where he offered himself up as a victim. For this is the eucharist: not only a commemorative service, but a reality; the presence of Jesus. It is useless to try to analyze this absolutely gratuitous mystery (as it would be silly to research for genius under the dissecting knife); we believe it on Jesus' word. On the other hand, we are not talking about a new sacrifice being performed on the altar, either. No, that was accomplished once and for all on Calvary. It cannot be begun again. But the eucharist is this sacrifice of Calvary gone beyond time and space, coming before us in order for us to participate in it.

Because of this, the mission of the priest is likewise

to help others to enter into the saving sacrifice of Christ. For it is certainly possible to attend a eucharist without ever really entering into the sacrifice of Christ, or to do so only halfheartedly. We too easily divide our lives into two compartments: one contains religion, devotion, prayer; the other, family, business, friendships, recreation. Between the two we set up a secure barrier. We refuse to let the gospel and Christian morality affect the real problems in our life. But such an attitude is absolutely false! Our whole life — our problems, questions of conscience, temptations, involvements — should be brought into the eucharist to be saturated with the divine. In this sphere the priest has an indispensible role to play in challenging our preconceptions and teaching us to be more open.

Whenever the Christian thus desires to receive communion during a eucharist, he should not forget that to unite himself with the victim on Calvary is to let himself be borne along by this current of generosity. Christ offered himself, gave himself up for us. The priest recalls this to himself in the ritual of the "breaking of the bread": he breaks the one bread to make several parts. The eucharist is love being given in sharing. It is impossible to remain locked in one's selfishness; the eucharist is "shared bread."

***

The Eucharist: One Heart, One Spirit

In The Eucharist, Christians Gathered Around Their Priests Are United In One Heart, One Spirit; They Nourish Their Faith And Sing Their Hope As A Resurrected People.

The priestly mission to bring the unique sacrifice of the saving Christ before the men and women of all times and all nations is accomplished in the celebration of a solemn family meal. For the eucharist is also the Christian assembly, the gathering of those who have put their hope in Christ. It has its origin in the ritual meal of the Jewish Passover during which Jesus consecrated bread and wine. To gather for the eucharist is to sit at the table together, with no distinction of race or social status. In choosing bread and wine, Christ expressed his preference for ordinary, everyday food appreciated by the poorest of men and women: those people who know the real taste of bread and who thirst for a wine that can give them strength. It is important to note that Jesus never spoke of a eucharist until after he had nourished the hungry crowds.

The priest, consecrated and delegated from among the people of God for this service at the altar, also has the duty and the mission to strengthen love and unity among the members of the community for which he is responsible. We don't think enough about this truth: the divine life which animates Christians from the moment of their baptism, and which the eucharist preserves and develops, makes them more brother and sister to one another than the closest family ties. In spite of themselves they can be divided by wars, social struggles, race or skin color, or even geographic necessity; but that does not interfere with their membership in the same great international family: that of the children of the reign of God, sons and daughters of the one Father.

Everything in the eucharist recalls this unity of all Christians. The bread is made from many different grains of wheat ground in the same mill, kneaded to make one loaf. The wine is the product of a multitude of grapes trodden and pressed together. These are symbols of unity. All those who are of Christ are members of one great body of which he is the head. The reading of the letters of the first companions of Christ, the remembrance of the saints who founded and spread the church, the sharing of news about Christians spread all over the earth, prayers for those not present, the mention of the dead of the community, the communion songs and acclamations — these are all signs of a great family reunion. Whenever the eucharist is celebrated, whether in the most ornate of cathedrals or the humblest of country churches, in a papal basilica with all its pomp and splendor or undercover in a refugee camp with a tin cup for a chalice, it is always the same people of God meeting in the presence of Christ.

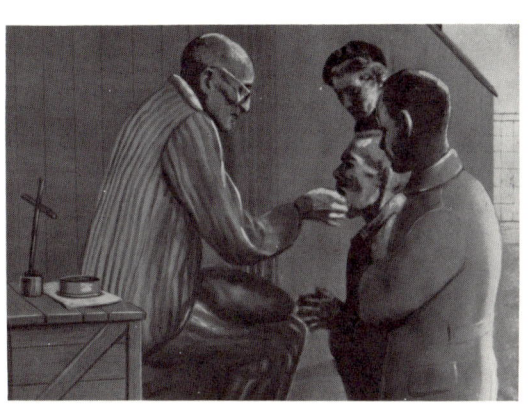

It is the priest's role to see that Christians assembling for the eucharist never give the scandal of a disunited family, for they would no longer be "one heart and one spirit." Nothing is more sad than a eucharist where people come for communion, to "break bread" together, while trying to remain uninvolved with those around them like people sitting bored in a waiting room or silent in a movie theatre.

Finally, while the priest is consecrated to the ministry of reconciliation between sinful humanity and its God by his vocation, he nevertheless presides over the Christian assembly in a festive spirit. The eucharist is surely a sacrifice; but it must be remembered that its victim is the risen Christ. So why should Christians be mournful when they gather? They know they are loved by God, members of his family, dwellers in Paradise. Their life on earth has a meaning. They can thus sing their joy and their hope in magnificent choirs, shout out triumphant "Alleluias" to the sound of organs and bells, decorate their churches in splendor to the honor of God, dress their ministers in joyful vestments, and unfold their jubilant liturgies in repeating: "Alleluia! We were dead because of our faults; God has raised us up with Christ; with him we live again."

The Universal Celebration

When The Priest Celebrates The Eucharist, He Does So With The Entire Universe.

Minister of the resurrection — with this theme we must conclude our look at the priest's role of service to God and man. It is important to mention because the priest is also bound to remind Christians that they should never lack optimism, never lead a sad and gloomy life, never shrink back before death. Because at the bottom of their being they have already gone from real death (their separation from God in sin) to real life (their entrance into divine life). Like everyone else they can still experience terrible moments as they end their earthly existence; but they should know that their new life, their divine life, continues forever.

As minister of the resurrection, the priest follows Paul the apostle in recalling to Christians that if Christ is risen from the dead, they too will rise from the dead in their turn. Divine energy will transfigure their bodies, whether these are lying intact in a tomb or are ashes scattered to the four winds. They will be recovered from the fleshly existence they had on earth, and all in them that was limited by time and space will be transformed; no more suffering, mourning, or tears.

In addition, since the body of Christ belonged to this creation, lived and was rooted in it, and is now transfigured and glorified, we can say that the whole world is associated to him and is likewise called to glorification and transfiguration. So that with the resurrection of Christ the entire cosmos finds all its beauty in the original plan of God. It's already done; it's a sure thing. But it is for man, made lord of creation by God, to give his free assent to this.

It is the vocation of a priest to carry this deep yearning in his prayer and to help men and women to leave behind their sinful mentality in order to render themselves to God; then nature's own transfiguration can commence, bringing the whole of nature, animal, vegetable and mineral, all technical and scientific advances under the reign of God. Creation, instead of being at the service of evil, being used for the destruction and sabotage of true values, for the loss of minds and hearts, will serve the good — to the honor of God, the salvation of men, and the fulfillment of the whole universe.

This is then the priest's struggle as well. Far from leaving behind the world, creation, and progress, he must do everything to snatch them from the domination of evil. And he is confident; because Christ has risen, Easter is assured for the entire universe. When the priest celebrates the eucharist, he celebrates with the universe itself.

PART THREE

chapter one
Come One, Come All

Among those he gathered to himself Jesus chose mature confident men emboldened by a religious vision; but very different in character, opinion, and social status.

The time has come to ask ourselves how the companions of Jesus were recruited and called. For out of hundreds of men won over by his teaching, healings, and expressions of intimacy with his Father, he chose only a small number of close friends.

These close companions were all mature men, except perhaps for someone like John who seems to have been younger (he was probably around twenty or so). They all had an occupation, with all its responsibilities and risks. They were all involved in the great problems of their people and their time. Before choosing them, Jesus spent a night in prayer and reflection atop a mountain in order to indicate that God directed this choice.

The elect were all from the region of Galilee; but from very different, even conflicting, classes and mentalities. Peter, Andrew, James, and John all formed his first small group, to which later were added Phillip and Bartholomew-Nathaniel, also found around John the Baptist. On the side of the ardent nationalists there were many zealots ("terrorists" we would call them today), that is to say, fierce partisans for national independence who pushed for a war of liberation — carried out essentially through assassinations — against the occupying army; here were found Simon the zealot and Judas Iscariot. Several others, on the contrary, were "collaborators" in the real sense of the word; they believed in a negotiated settlement with the Romans occupying the country, and therefore profited from the existing regime: men like Matthew the publican and maybe the other James who could have been his brother. There was also Thomas who we know was very down to earth but not too caught up in things; he always demanded proof, to be able to see things with his own eyes before believing them. Finally, there was a certain Thaddeus whose name might signify "the man with guts," which was perhaps a surname to indicate that this was a giant of a man with great physical strength.

In brief, this was a collection of restless and stubborn Galileans who could probably never agree on anything. They sometimes even fought among themselves over questions of rank and prestige.

But it would be a mistake to think that they were mostly ignorant country bumpkins. Jesus could certainly have chosen either beggars or aristocrats to accompany him; but for the most part he chose men from between the extremes, men who had an occupation, had had some schooling, were very interested in politics and business, knew their Bible and had a religious sense.

On The Road To Damascus The Persecutor Was Conquered And Seized By His Victim: It Was A Total Reversal: Paul Became The Greatest Apostle Of Christ.

Later on, after his resurrection, Jesus appeared to the most rabid of his persecutors and called him to follow him, thus signifying that there was no limit to the breadth of his call.

The story of this unexpected and amazing reversal is written in the book of the first days of the church, called "The Acts of the Apostles." A fanatic observer of the religious law of Moses, Paul the Pharisee had never met Jesus; as a matter of fact he had been away from Palestine during the two or three years Jesus walked the roads of Galilee and Judea proclaiming the reign of God, before going to his passion. But when he returned to Jerusalem, Paul learned of the very vital fraternities or communes of Jesus' disciples and discovered a whole new current of religious ideas which threatened to wash away the established religious order. He passionately followed the legal case begun against Steven, a disciple of Jesus. Steven, inspired by an unshakeable faith in Christ and graced with a remarkable eloquence and mastery of foreign tongues, had created an atmosphere very favorable to the first fraternities in the city. Well-versed in the study of scripture and citing the recent facts of the condemnation of Jesus, he confounded the judges with ease and did not hesitate to accuse them of betraying God's will themselves. The outrage of the High Court led to his being dragged outside the walls of the city to be stoned to death. Paul participated in his execution; he heard Steven

The story of Steven's death is in the Book of the Acts of the Apostles, chapter 8 (verses 55 to 60).

cry out as he fell beneath the hail of stones striking him in the face, "Lord Jesus, don't hold my death against these people."

This scene and these words would not leave Paul's memory and followed him incessantly. But he hardened his heart, he resisted; and, the better to blind himself to this reality, he asked to be sent on a search through the cities of the province to arrest the disciples of this famous Jesus and to lead them in bonds before the tribunal in Jerusalem.

So there he was, off to Damascus, never expecting that someone awaited him on the road. But who?

In truth, another struggle had been raging within him for some time. The sight of Steven, battered and praying for his enemies as he died, was always with him. When you got down to it, who was he really persecuting? Who was he after? Disciples like this Steven? Or the master of them all, Jesus himself? Wasn't it Jesus being crucified anew in the person of his friends?

And this is exactly what Jesus brought him to see in his vision on the road to Damascus, an overpowering vision of the risen Christ: "Paul, Paul! Why are you persecuting me?"

The account of Paul's conversion is in chapter 9 of the Acts of the Apostles.

"But who are you, speaking to me?"

"I am Jesus whom you are persecuting."

Paul was overwhelmed. But he felt a twinge of stubbornness, like a horse who rears up when spurred, refusing to go forward in spite of the continuing pain:

"Ah, Paul, you rebel against me. And yet..."

The rabid persecutor saw himself conquered. In the middle of his flight he was pinned, as if irresistibly caught by the neck. And he imagined that all his person was changing, transforming itself into another: it was as if his very skin were being replaced. He came around, he gave himself up, he abandoned himself; for the last thing he wanted in his life was to oppose himself to the will of God.

"Lord, what would you have me do?"

"Go into the city; there someone will tell you what you must do."

Meanwhile, the small fraternity of Christians in Damascus had heard that Paul was coming armed with a warrant for the arrest of all those who followed Christ. But it was also rumored that this Paul was undecided and that he wanted to meet some authentic Christians for a worthwhile exchange of views.

Ananias, the leader of the community of Jesus' disciples, was very anxious about the whole thing. To go find Paul was like walking into a trap, wasn't it? But to refuse to talk with him was to show his lack of faith in Christ whose power to change hearts was limitless. What if Paul's heart was really ready; if he could give himself over to God, who like a potter could make a thing of great beauty from an ugly lump of clay? Ananias understood that Jesus was calling him to make their first steps toward Paul.

"Paul, my brother, Jesus sent me to you so that you might see clearly and be filled with the spirit of God."

No more was necessary for Paul to be truly enlightened and to understand all that remained for him to do. We could say that it was like scales falling from his eyes. From here on he was another man; he soon requested baptism. Paul had heard the call of God; he would become the greatest apostle the church would ever know.

REFLECTIONS

When Christ Calls People To Follow Him, He Sees No Importance In The Distinctions Men Set Up Among Themselves: Age, Wealth, Race, Culture Or Class. One Man Is As Good As Another In This Perspective, Which Is God's Point of View.

We have just seen how Christ takes one man from work with his nets, another from his tax booth, a persecutor in all his rage — all to manifest the freedom of his choice and the power of his grace. With this he wanted to express the mystery of love he carried within himself.

You, reader, who are perhaps asking yourself whether Christ hasn't entered your life to have you hear his call, you can only be encouraged and reassured by these accounts of "calling" taken from the scriptures.

First of all, as you can see, Jesus did not start his church with children and adolescents, but with mature men, young men earning a living and deeply caught up in the great social, political and religious problems of their country and their time. Maybe we should say then that vocations from among young men and adults are the most appropriate, considering the functions of the priesthood, this bridge of salvation stretched between a sinful humankind and its God. This is true even if some men hear a call from God beginning in their early youth. At all times, at every age, Christ can invite you to follow him.

On the other hand, these so-called values and distinctions which men put between themselves in line with the thought and judgement of the kingdoms of the earth have no force whatever in this new manner of seeing and weighing men and things which the reign of God offers. Merely human considerations, envisaged outside the sight of God and the light cast on all things by the divine Spirit, count for nothing at all.

This is what God made the prophet Samuel understand on the day several thousand years before Christ when the old man went out to find a new leader for the Hebrew people. Arriving among the family of one Jesse of Bethlehem, Samuel was struck by his oldest son, a great block of a man, and said to himself, "Surely he's the one God has chosen; I have his elect before me!" But he remembered that Saul, the decadent king he was replacing, had also impressed him once with his great stature and his fine bearing. And God made him understand: "Do not consider his exterior virtues, for I have looked over him. The sight of God is not the sight of man. Man looks at appearances; but God looks at the heart."

This account is in chapter 16 of the Book of Samuel.

In the end, it was young David, the eighth and last son of Jesse, who was God's choice. David, a young man who wasn't even presented to the prophet, but remained in the fields watching over the flocks; who in the eyes of his father was almost an afterthought among the family. And it was he who would be anointed at the hands of the prophet.

The young officer Charles de Foucauld led a carefree and joyous life.

Converted and ordained a priest, Father de Foucauld became a hermit in the Sahara desert.

God chooses whom he wills. This is what Paul, the converted persecutor, came to understand; Paul who considered himself nothing compared with the first companions of Jesus. One day he wrote to the Christian community in Corinth: "Recall the circumstances of your conversion to Christ and where you found yourself at the moment you were called. There are not many cultivated people among you, nor influential or well-born persons. But those who are seen as little people are the ones God seeks out to confound those who boast of their knowledge, and those seen as weak and defenseless, to confuse those who vaunt their power. These 'nobodies,' these are the people God has chosen to bring shame upon those who consider themselves 'something.' For he wants not a single creature on earth to glory in itself and thereby grasp at any title whatever in his eyes."

A passage drawn from the First Letter of Paul to the Christians at Corinth, chapter 1 (verses 26 to 31).

We must therefore assert very strongly: no considerations of birth, fortune, race, social status or culture can be decisive for a vocation to the priesthood.

In the history of the church we see that Christ called men to follow him from every social class: sons of great, wealthy families like Francis of Assisi; military men like Ignatius of Loyola; the sons of poor peasants like Pope John XXIII; playboys and big spenders before their conversions, like Charles de Foucault; thinkers like Teilhard de Chardin; people less well-suited for studies like the Cure of Ars.

In the present day, with the expansion of Christianity throughout the world, men of all races and colors have entered the priesthood. This is surely the full realization of Jesus' last command to his disciples: "Go around the world and make disciples in all nations!"

The birthplace and family home of Pope John XXIII.

chapter two
In Spite of Their Faults

In spite of their zeal and generosity and the three years they lived close at his side, Jesus' companions kept their dreams and their prejudices, their violent instincts and their ambitions, their rivalries and their meanness.

The companions Jesus chose to follow him came from different social backgrounds and had different ways of thinking about things. But they also had their own distinctive personalities, and in some cases were not easy to live with. Jesus often suffered from their lack of understanding, their prejudice, their instinct for violence, their rivalries and ambitions, their flushes of enthusiasm and their fervid affirmations of loyalty which were most often followed by pettiness and abandonment. He loved them all the same; and like a great teacher, he pursued without interruption their formation for their future priestly role in the context of daily events and happenings.

One day Jesus wanted to go up from Galilee to Jerusalem, and his small group of friends decided to take the short cut through Samaritan territory. But in one village they were refused passage.

<small>This account is in chapter 9 of Luke's Gospel (verses 51 to 56).</small>

Enraged, the two brothers James and John told Jesus, "You should call down fire from heaven to incinerate this village and its inhabitants. That would show them!"

"What! You dare to speak like that! You don't know what spirit you're listening to."

If they could only have recognized that it was the spirit of vengeance and willful power which spoke in them..., yet Jesus had himself come to win hearts through kindness, in granting them forgiveness. Hearts might very well yield before force; but they would not open. Men had been created free: there was their worth and their dignity. God respects them in this, their greatness. Hearts are not won over in banging heads around.

***

Even with their good teacher, the companions would keep their all too human ideas until the last possible day. They thought that it was in establishing a new political regime, through revolution and a coup d'etat if necessary, that God's rights would finally be recognized. Jesus with his incredible powers seemed able to overthrow any army and wipe out all the wrongdoers on earth. He was holding off for now, but he undoubtedly had a secret plan. The Day would come and he would go into action; they, his faithful companions, would occupy the top posts in his new regime.

This is what they talked about, a couple of paces behind Jesus' back, as they walked the roads of Palestine. Since they dared not themselves express their secret ambitions to Jesus, the two hotheads among them, James and John, one day asked their mother to speak for them. She sometimes went along with the caravan of Jesus' intimates and was of great service to the small wandering community. So there she found herself, prostrate before Jesus' feet with a look of supplication. Her two sons stood nearby. They wanted Jesus to grant their request even before he knew what they were asking: "Master, promise us that you'll grant what our mother asks."

But Jesus wasn't happy with this at all: "Look, what do you want?" So the mother explained her request: "Promise me that my sons here will have the highest places at your side on the day of your triumph" (she meant to refer to the new regime she thought he was going to establish).

"You really don't have any idea what you're asking for," Jesus responded to James and John. "Are you first willing to drink the bitter cup of suffering I must drink? To go all the way with me in my misery?"

"Sure, we're ready for anything."

"That's true, one day you will know my suffering,"

Jesus replied as he thought of their future. "But as for what you ask, that is my Father's business."

James and John were ambitious and naïve. They hoped for human success in the kingdom of God. It was a big mistake; but they easily realized this and tried to make amends, for they passionately loved Christ.

It was another story with Judas; but we've already gone into that. He didn't resist the temptations of wealth and power. He betrayed Jesus out of spite.

This account is found in Mark's Gospel, chapter 10 (verses 35 to 41), and in Matthew's Gospel, Chapter 20 (verses 20 to 24).

***

One day when Jesus said he was going to visit his sick friend Lazarus at Bethany, they pointed out to him the dangers of traveling so near Jerusalem: "Master, not so long ago they were still talking about stoning you over there; and now you want to go back."

But Jesus had made up his mind. Then Thomas, trying to look courageous, shouted out for all the others, "Well, let's get going, then. We'll show them that we're ready to die with him!"

Somewhat later, however, on the night of his arrest in the Garden of Olives, they all abandoned him and took off, seeing that he was allowing himself to be arrested.

***

Yet Jesus had forewarned them. On the road going up to this Garden of Olives he told them, "This very night you will all lose courage when you see what will happen. The words of the prophet stick in my mind: 'I will strike down the shepherd and the flock will scatter.'"

Peter, thinking that Jesus was just going through a moment of pessimism and was painting an unjustifiably bleak picture of treason and abandonment by his best friends, raised his voice in protest: "Even when all the others have left you, I'll still be here. As you see me standing here, I am determined to stick with you through prison and death. Yes; I'm ready to give my life for you."

These words of Jesus to Peter are found in Matthew, chapter 26 (verses 31 to 35), and John, chapter 13 (verses 36 to 38).

"Peter, you say that you're ready to give your life for me. But I tell you that today, this very night, the rooster will not have crowed twice before you have said three times that you do not know me."

Peter would hear nothing of this: "Me, deny you! They'd have to kill me first."

But later that night after Jesus had been arrested in the Garden of Olives, Peter and John followed the band of soldiers as they led him away. They managed to sneak into the courtyard of the tribunal where Jesus was being held, anxious to find out what would happen to him. Peter went up to a group of soldiers warming themselves around a small

fire in the corner of the yard. In the dim light of the flames, one of the servants recognized him and pointed him out, saying, "You there. You're part of this Jesus gang too, aren't you?" Peter was terrified and tried to act dumb: "Who? Don't know'em. What's that you say?" But she insisted, shaking her finger at him, "Hey, look! Here's one of them over here!" "But I told you, I don't know that man!"

Dawn was breaking; and nearby a rooster started to crow.

Now the soldiers were beginning to be suspicious of him. "Hey, listen," they said, "for sure you're one of his supporters. Anyway, your accent is Galilean, like his. You give yourself away when you talk." "I think I remember him," another one said. "Weren't you in the garden with him tonight?"

Peter thought it was all over. He started to curse and swear (and "swear" meant something like: " 'God almighty, let me be struck down if I'm lying' "). He shouted, "I told you I never knew the man you're talking about!"

This account is in Luke, chapter 22; Mark, chapter 14; Matthew, chapter 26; John, chapter 18.

They let him be. Soon a loud cry broke through the night; the rooster crowed once more. Peter then remembered what Jesus told him: "This very night, before the rooster crows twice, you will have denied me three times." He ran out of the courtyard and burst into tears.

When Love For Christ And Passion For the Reign Of God Overcome All Weakness and Fear.

Jesus had nevertheless entrusted Peter with great responsibilities, ever since the day they had met on the shores of Galilee and he called him to follow. Peter had been the leader of a small team of fishermen; so he still had some authority over the rest of the group. Jesus at one time called him "Peter," which means "rock" or "boulder." The name stuck to him since that time, although no one knew why, exactly. Then one day Jesus explained: "I call you Peter because I will build my church on this rock that you are; and the forces of evil will never be able to shake you." To be sure, Jesus confided his church to all twelve companions taken as a group; but they were not a group unless they remained united with their leader who was named Simon Peter. He was the "bedrock" which guaranteed the soundness and cohesion of the structure, the community.

These words of Jesus are found in Matthew's Gospel, chapter 16 (verses 13 to 19).

On other occasions, too, Jesus confided supreme responsibility for his future church to Peter, as well as all its powers.

But Peter did not measure up to the trust placed in him and had denied his master.

After his resurrection, Jesus was to reconfirm Peter in the eyes of his companions, in a touching and conclusive way. This is how it happened:

Peter and five others had gone out one night to fish on the Sea of Galilee. They worked through the night without taking anything in their nets. As they turned their boat toward shore feeling both disappointment and fatigue, they caught sight of a man who seemed to be waiting for them. Taking him for a merchant or traveler, they were not too surprised to hear him shout, "Hey, you hard workers! Catch any fish?" "No, nothing at all," they replied. "Listen to me: cast your nets to your right and you'll find something!"

They thought that maybe he had seen a couple of fish breaking the surface of the water as he watched them from the shoreline. And since fish swim in schools, well, maybe he was right. In any case they were angry about coming back empty-handed and were ready to give it one last try. They let out a long net at the place he indicated.

But when they tried to pull it in they found it so heavy with fish that this was impossible. At that moment John, who was among them in the boat, suddenly remembered another miraculous catch. He was thus certain that this stranger on shore was Jesus himself. He turned to Peter who was struggling with the net and cried, "It's the Lord!"

This account is found in John's Gospel, chapter 21.

At these words Peter understood also. He dropped the net, quickly gathered up the clothes he had taken off during his work, and jumped in the water to reach Jesus even sooner.

The boat was about a hundred yards from shore, and the others rowed toward it as they pulled in their net loaded with fish.

When they set their feet on land, they found Jesus sitting next to a small wood fire with bread already prepared at his side. "Bring me some of those fish you've just caught," he said. He cooked them over the fire and then said to the others, "And now, come over here and eat with me."

Not one of them was clumsy enough to break the silence during their modest meal; they all recognized him and that was enough. They let themselves be served. Jesus himself divided the bread and fish among them. It all happened in a calm atmosphere of simplicity and warmth, there at the side of the lake beneath the rising sun.

Once they had finished, Jesus turned to Peter and said, "Peter, do you love me more than the others do?" What an odd question it seemed. Peter was a little embarrassed. Of course he loved Jesus! But more than the others? This was not an easy question to answer. He remembered his foolish protestations of loyalty just a few hours before Jesus' arrest — then the courtyard, the small fire, the servant, and the rooster's crow.

He answered hesitantly, "Lord, you know that I love you." Jesus renewed his question: "Peter, are you sure you love me?" A little bothered with this insistence, Peter responded brusquely, "Of course I do." A third time Jesus asked him, "Peter, do you really love me?" And Peter started to worry.

Jesus didn't trust his love! But he had denied Jesus three times, after all: this small fire on the beach reminded him so much of the fire in the courtyard that night. Peter was nearly in tears as he saw how Jesus had reason to doubt his affection. And yet this time he was ready to give his life to make good his disloyalty. "Lord," he said, "you know everything; so you must know how I love you!"

And Jesus responded as he had to the two previous questions, "Then be the shepherd of my flock."

Jesus had already called himself the real, the only shepherd; that is to say, the real leader of all humankind. "I give my life for my sheep...; I know my sheep and my sheep know me...; I have other sheep which are not in this pasture; I lead them as well; they hear my voice. So there will be but one flock with only one shepherd."

<small>These words are found in chapter 10 of John's Gospel.</small>

Jesus confided his function as shepherd-king, protector of his human flock, to Peter for all time; he conferred on him a special and preeminent title among his other companions.

REFLECTIONS

God has chosen to need man!

As you read these pages you have perhaps stopped once or twice to reflect on the possibility of a personal call from God. And one of your reactions was probably: fine, that's all very nice. A priestly vocation is surely one of the best callings in the world. But how important it is! Could I possibly measure up to it? I shouldn't fool myself and rush into a decision on the spur of the moment. I know my own limits; I have a personality with shortcomings; I have my faults. I have sinful habits from which it is hard to free myself. I'm just not sure of myself. I can only respond by saying, "Lord, I'm weak and afraid of disappointing you!"

And this is how we truly stand before God. No one can say, "Lord, I am worthy." For the only true response is that of the centurion in the gospel: "Lord, I am not worthy."

Even the apostle Peter, before his presumptuous affirmations of loyalty, found himself prostrate at Jesus' feet one day in his boat saying, "Lord, go away from me; for I know I am nothing but a man with a heart full of sin!" This had been after the first miraculous catch he had taken on Jesus' command: "Peter, go out to the deep and cast your net." After seeing the result he understood the wide gulf that separated him from Jesus, as well as his own unworthiness to become the first among his companions. But Jesus had responded to him, "Even so, Peter, I will make you a fisher of men!"

This is how Jesus chose Peter, in spite of his uneven character and his freewheeling commitments followed close behind by lamentable defections; James and John in spite of their agressivity or Thomas in spite of his scepticism; even Judas in spite of his deranged love of power and money. They took the time to restrain these too-human reactions within them and opened themselves up to the new dimensions of the reign of God. One among them refused to do so and Jesus had to leave him behind. Like a good teacher, Jesus never wanted to do violence to their nature; he allowed his spirit to work in the depths of their hearts, counting all the while on their good will, their love for him, and their dedication to the reign of God.

In this way God wills to depend on men. It's a fact. But he gives them the utmost respect and violates no one's freedom. A person who has been grasped by Christ can always go back, can always give in to the temptations of the evil one.

Some people would like a perfect and faultless church. "We believe in God and Christ," they say, "but not in the church," because they dwell on the lives and behavior of her priests, of unworthy Christians. To think like this is to have understood nothing of the Christian religion, established precisely in order to "seek what was lost," to be the "friend of the scorned and despised," such as public sinners. The church will always be made up of human beings whose hearts are riddled with faults and full of weakness, as well as of men and women of great holiness. As in any human body, there will always be members in perfect health and others who are sick, paralyzed, deformed, cancerous. Yet the church still lives, and Christ still lives in his church.

Joan of Arc grasped this perfectly when she answered her inquisitioners demanding to know what difference she saw between Christ and the Church. "None," she stated simply. "For me they are one and the same." Yet the bishop questioning her was cunning and unworthy. He remained all the same a successor of the apostles with their power to consecrate other bishops and priests. Just like a fallen and convicted father who can still transmit life.

Jesus one day gave them this image of the reign of God: "It is like a very tiny seed becoming a great tree." This great tree is the church. It is always bursting forth with life, because Jesus lives in it. Yet we can see on it the traces of all kinds of wounds, different branches twisted, bruised, broken off in the storm; we can see tiny sprouts shooting out of its roots apart from the single trunk. This is the doing of bishops and priests, disunited

Sequoia or giant redwood in the Sierra Nevada, still alive after 2000 years. The tree is almost 500 feet high and a road runs through its trunk.

<small>This parable is found in Mark, chapter 4 (verses 30 to 32) and Matthew, chapter 13 (verses 31 and 32).</small>

Christians who are guilty of narrow vision, ambitious calculation, political maneuvering — and above all, guilty of a lack of love for one another. We have even seen a great rending of the church which continues to cause us suffering; yet in the spirit of the last Council, Christians are trying to heal the wounds of this division.

God wills to need men in spite of their faults and weaknesses. You recall how Christ agreed to be helped with his cross for a part of his way up to Calvary. The gospel tells us how the centurion in charge of the execution squad realized that Christ could not make it to Calvary on his own strength, weakened as he was from the torture. So he stopped a strong peasant on his way back from the fields, named Simon of Cyrene, and ordered him to relieve Jesus by carrying his crossbeam for a while. In this way Christ wanted a man just finishing his day's work to give him a hand at saving the world.

<small>This episode is recalled in the Gospels of Luke (chapter 23, verse 26), Mark (chapter 15, verse 21), and Matthew (chapter 27, verse 32).</small>

chapter three
To Take Up the Cross

Whoever wants to follow me should renounce himself and take up his cross.

Even though Jesus called men and used them to communicate his message and his person across nations and centuries, he could not admit people to his following who remained more enchanted with other things or other persons than with his kingdom.

This is the reason he warned his apostles against splendid processions and triumphal entries. He got them accustomed to totally different images, like that of a band of condemned men being led to their crucifixion while carrying their death on their shoulders. "I am going up to Jerusalem," he told them. "Waiting for me there are condemnation, torture, and death on a cross. Whoever wants to follow me should not be looking out for himself; instead let him take up his cross every day and go where I go."

"Taking up the cross" for Jesus' companions meant agreeing to live in contradiction with the idea of life adopted by the world which is opposed to the reign of God. Becoming a disciple and heir of a crucified man necessarily implies some renunciation.

> These words of Jesus are found in Luke's Gospel, chapter 14 (verse 27) and Matthew's Gospel, chapter 10 (verse 38).

Jesus once explained this to a man who generously offered him his services, saying, "Master, I'm ready to follow you anywhere." But Jesus warned him about momentary enthusiasm. Would this rash man be able to lead the wandering life of Jesus and his small group without any guarantees for tomorrow? "I warn you," he told him, "birds have their nests and foxes their dens; but I have nowhere to lay my head."

1. *The Companions of Jesus and Money.*

Another time there was a well-off young man full of idealism who heard Jesus preach the reign of God. He wanted this life of friendship with God more than anything else and was willing to pay any price to become part of it. He

> This account is in the Gospels, notably that of Mark, chapter 10 (verses 17 to 22).

was excited by this new way of looking at life in which the supreme value is to love as God loves us. Furthermore, he could honestly report to Jesus that all his life he had scrupulously observed the commandments of God as he had been taught them: he had never killed, never stolen; he had never committed adultery, never borne false witness, never wronged anyone, had always respected his parents and loved his neighbor as himself. "Am I lacking anything?" he asked Jesus.

The young man was sincere, and of truly beautiful spirit. Jesus regarded him intently. He loved this young man with a preferential love. Here was a member of the elite who could become one of his close companions. So he was going to offer him a higher degree of perfection than he had known before: that which was necessary for all those who agreed to follow him and become his apostles. "You only have to do one more thing to become perfect: sell all you have and give the money to the poor. In its place you will have gained a treasure in the reign of God. Then come and follow me."

But he would not be around for that; he was utterly crushed. He was very wealthy and owned much property. He went away very sad.

Here was a young man without the courage to break with everything that had helped him to lead a good life up until then. In all his comfort, graced with a good and kind nature, the beneficiary of a good education, he had never known the problems faced by working people trying to live an honest life. He had perhaps never seen any drunkenness, theft, or lying in his environment; brought up in a closed world, he had instead grown in respect for the religious law. He didn't have the willpower needed to break with his middle-class comfort; the new life held out to him seemed impossible; easier, perhaps, for common folk like Jesus' companions who were used to not having enough to eat and sleeping on hard ground. He returned home.

Jesus watched the rich young man leaving with his head hung in sadness and concluded, "How difficult it is for a rich man to enter the reign of God!" How much more true if he were invited to become one of Jesus' close companions, a successor!

In the same way, when he sent his companions out on missions to preach the reign of God, it was Jesus' custom to instruct them in an absolute lack of concern for their own reward. He would grant them incredible powers over sickness in order to help them in their preaching, but he never wanted them to receive anything in exchange: "You have freely received; give freely!" Since they were going to preach about renunciation, it was fitting for them to provide an example of it. People leaving on a trip would usually take certain precautions: for instance, carrying along some pieces of gold or silver which could easily be hidden in a moneybelt or on one's person; checking the leather straps on one's backpack; making sure to bring along two cloaks, a light one for the day and a heavier one for night; wearing heavy, leather sandals for the road. But Jesus wanted to train his companions in a life of detachment and counseled them: "Take nothing with you for your journey: neither gold, nor silver, nor coins hidden in your belt; take no pack, no supplies, not even a stick; and wear no sandals for your road." How would they survive? He assured them that their preaching would surely merit food and clothing from hearts seeking God: "Remember that the laborer has a right to his sustenance."

These instructions for going out on mission are found in the Gospels, notably those of Matthew (chapter 10) and Luke (chapter 10).

The reign of God thus requires an absolute disinterest. Anyone too attached to money, comfort and an easy life must truly give them up in order to follow Christ.

2. *The Companions of Jesus and Bonds of the Heart.*

In the same way, too great an attachment to the ways of the flesh or to family affections can be an obstacle to the vocation of an apostle.

Noticing someone in the group listening to the proclamation of the reign of God, Jesus called to him as to many others, "Come, follow me!" But he hesitated, saying, "Gladly, but first I have to wait for my father's death."

In Luke's Gospel, chapter 9 (verses 57 to 62), we find an account of several callings.

Jesus replied to him with a note of sarcasm, "Let the dead bury their dead. You are going to proclaim the reign of God." There are some cases when a person who feels truly called must know how to break his family ties; when, for instance, the family situation is shut against any spiritual reality, when it remains locked in a way of thinking, judging and living based on a worldly model dominated by the law of sin, when it refuses to be opened to the new ways of living of the reign of God which are based on the love God has for men — in short, when it is "dead" to the new dimensions of life brought by Christ.

One day when Jesus found himself in a house surrounded by a crowd trying to hear him, he received word that his mother and cousins were outside and wanted to speak with him. He replied, "My mother and my brothers are those who hear the word of God and do what he says." Beneath the apparent harshness of his expression, he wanted the others to understand that men are closer to him in their hearts and their adherence to the will of God than in ties of blood or family.

On another occasion a truly warm individual came up and said to Jesus, "I have decided to follow you. But first let me go say farewell to my family."

Jesus, who knows the hearts of men, was aware that this man was sincere and a little timid. If he returned to his family he ran the risk of being overwhelmed once more by the affection that they might have toward one or another there and would probably not have the strength to pull himself out of it. Standing there on the road that day, they could see a peasant in an adjoining field beginning to plow; never looking behind him, he kept his eyes on a point in the distance in order to keep plowing in a straight line. In the same way, once we start something we shouldn't too often try to rehash the whole business. "Whoever puts his hand to the plow," replied Jesus, "and stops to look behind is not made to work for the reign of God."

These words are found in Luke's Gospel, chapter 14 (verses 25 to 33).

Still others wanted to join him. He warned them and did not hesitate to set out his requirements: "If there are those who want to follow me and don't feel they can choose me over their father or mother, spouse or children, and are not ready to die for me, then it is of no use; they cannot follow me." This is the reason it is important to think this over. It's no use to throw oneself into the fires of enthusiasm only to abandon the whole thing soon after. "When you want to build something," Jesus continued, "you start by sitting down and figuring what your expenses will be; you take account of everything you've got, to be sure you will be able to complete the task. Otherwise, if you are forced to stop once you have laid only the foundations, people will laugh, saying, 'Look at that! He started building and only got as far as the cellar!' So you should think it over well. If you want to follow me, remember that you must be able to give up everything you hold dear."

3. The Companions of Jesus and Life in a Group.

The brothers James and John had agreed to leave their family behind to follow Jesus. After returning with a miraculous and unexpected catch taken under Jesus' direction following a night of fruitless labor on the lake, they made up their minds freely and in full awareness of their motives. Leaving their father Zebedee with the boat and all their nets, they followed Jesus intending never to leave him.

Mark's Gospel, chapter 1 (verses 19 and 20).

In thus breaking their links with their loved ones and the tools of their trade, they knew they were also giving up the independent life of skilled fishermen. Until then they were part of a small group of friends grouped around Peter as the head of their small fishing cooperative. From now on they would be integrated into a wider and more diverse grouping of companions. They would have to live with collaborators like Matthew, even though they were ardent nationalists; with cool, rational sceptics like Thomas, though they were hot-blooded; with puzzling and calculating men like Judas, though they were spontaneous and generous. This was truly a way of renouncing the freedom to live their own life and their own dreams, and thus another way to carry their own cross, as Jesus had said.

Jesus clearly intended to gather such a diverse group of men to found his church. It reflected the image of a world amazingly varied in its peoples, a world into which these men would be thrown as leaven into a lump of dough.

Living together as they traveled the dusty roads of Palestine, the companions had to learn to know, respect and accept one another, to complement each other and to form a real unity, all in dedicating themselves to the common work

Luke's Gospel, chapter 9; Matthew's Gospel, chapter 17.

of proclaiming the coming of the reign of God. Whenever possible, Jesus sent them out on missions two by two. There would be practically no "best friends" among them, nor any special concern for one in preference to another. But when he wanted to take them further into the secret of his mission or his own person, Jesus would meet together with three of them at once: Peter, James and John. As members of a smaller group, these three men would have the privilege of accompanying Jesus up the mountain to share a vision of his divine glory; they would then be prepared to see him later on, prostrate in agony in the Garden of Olives, before his sacrifice on Calvary. Afterwards, they would be able to bear irrefutable witness about these occurrences in the group.

Mark's Gospel, chapter 14; Matthew's Gospel, chapter 26.

Such was Jesus' real desire that his companions get together in a very tight community once they had decided to follow him. He spent his brightest days with them teaching them how to pray, showing them the deep meaning of the public teaching he offered in the form of a parable and comparison, explaining the writings of Moses and the prophets and how they were related to the events the group was living together. And it was with a group of two men that he walked on the road to Emmaus that Easter night, speaking with such authority about the scriptures which concerned him, the Messiah, before finally making himself known by the "breaking of the bread." Surrounded by the community of his twelve most intimate friends he ate his farewell meal; in the midst of the same group he appeared suddenly following his resurrection — and again, eight days later when the presence of Thomas completed the group, he was present to them once more. Whenever he had a lesson to give or a re-

Luke's Gospel, chapter 24.

John's Gospel, chapter 20.

proach to make to one of them, he always spoke to them in community, in the presence of them all.

Jesus esteemed the life of the community so highly that he placed the destiny of his church in the hands of the twelve gathered together, promising to be with them until the end of the world.

The night of his arrest, as he spoke to them one last time, he said: "Father, I pray for them. Let them be one as you and I are one. Let them be joined in a common life so that when the world sees them thus it will be sure that you sent me on earth."

> These words are found in John's Gospel, chapter 17 (verses 20 to 23).

If Jesus expressed this desire and this prayer with such fervor, it was because group life, life in community, is indispensible for the achievement of salvation for the whole race of men; and as such, it implies renunciation of certain things and makes clear demands. But it also assures a kind of effectiveness in its goal of obtaining fulfillment for each of its members.

***

In fact, alongside the days of friendly life together, the community of Jesus' companions knew its days of grayness and shadow; for it is true that the heart of man is always threatened and besieged by the evil one and often makes hidden compromises with him. As pettiness met the light of day, interior rivalries and conflicts erupted. James and John, as we saw above, had ambitions to be at Jesus' side in seats of power which they imagined would be part of the establishment of his new kingdom. The very night of his farewell meal, as they felt the ultimate importance of these final hours, Jesus' companions fought among themselves over who would occupy the best seats at the table, each one boasting of his titles and office in the group. So Jesus had to stoop to washing their feet to teach them a lesson: "If I, the one you call Master, wash your feet, it is to show you that you in turn should wash one another's feet." That is to say that in the very heart of their group they should witness to a love which stops at nothing — not jealousy, not mistrust, not rancor, not pettiness. For that love is the very existence of the community.

> These words of Christ are found in John's Gospel, chapter 13 (verses 12 to 17).

Among those whose feet Jesus had just washed was Judas. He left the heart of this community of Jesus' companions and instead decided in secret to betray the Christ and go over to his enemies. Jesus did not hesitate to let the group know of this defection and the foul machinations of one of its members: "I must tell you all: one of you will betray me. Yes, I tell you, one of you eating here at this table with me." At this declaration, everyone stopped eating and looked around. These words of Jesus echoed like

> This account is found in the Gospel of the apostle John, chapter 13 (verses 21 to 30), and in the Gospel of the apostle Matthew, chapter 26 (verses 21 to 24).

thunder; everyone was astonished. Since they knew Jesus' words were infallible and had learned to be critical even of themselves, they asked one another, "Is it me he's talking about?" When Judas turned to ask this question himself, Jesus replied, "You know that it is you"; but he did so with such gentleness that the others could not hear what he said. Peter felt responsible for all of the group and wanted at all costs to know whom Jesus was speaking of. So he motioned to John who was sitting next to Jesus and said, "Try to find out who he means"; perhaps he would be able to stop the traitor in time. All the men were stretched out on long couches around the table, so it was no trouble for John to lean over, put his head on Jesus' chest and ask quietly, "Lord, tell me: who is it?" He wanted to know the secret. And Jesus would tell him; for it was necessary to have at least one member of the community who could testify later that, at that moment, Jesus had read the heart of the hypocrite. He whispered to John without even pronouncing the name of the man about to do evil, "It's the one who will take this bread that I dip." He thus took a piece of bread, dipped it in the sauce on his plate and offered it to Judas. This was a sign of great honor, to offer such bread to a guest, like the modern custom of drinking to someone's health; it was above all a sign of friendship, a last call. Judas took the bread, but was wrapped up in his hate and his stubbornness. Jesus then said to him, "Do what you're going to do quickly." It was better to get it over with and not pretend any longer. No one in the group knew what he was referring to; Judas was the treasurer and everyone thought Jesus had told him to buy something for the next day's feast or to give something to the poor as was the custom with the Passover feast. They saw Judas leave and cover himself with the night.

A striking and upsetting scene from the community life of Jesus' companions. We have not finished discovering all its meaning and significance... .

***

Some months later as he assumed the destiny of the young Church, Peter would preoccupy himself to the exclusion of all else with replacing the renegade member of the group (Judas had hanged himself). Matthias would be elected the twelfth apostle. Peter had understood the importance and the necessities of the community/church in bringing to fulfillment the salvation of humankind.

> This episode is recounted in the Book of the Acts of the Apostles, chapter 1.

4. The Companions of Jesus and Total Commitment.

If internal difficulties leading to both abandonment and treason could be found within the community of companions itself, what could be expected from the hostile world of the kingdoms of earth where the companions had to live and proclaim the law of love of the reign of God!

Jesus warned those who wanted to follow him: "Don't think that I have come to bring ease and peace of mind on earth; say, rather, that I have brought you combat. And remember that the disciple is no greater than his master. If the world hates you, know that it hated me before you. It follows; if you were still in the world, the world would love you as it loves all those who live in its way. But you have another spirit, and that is why the world hates you. Since they persecuted me, they will persecute you, too; as they spied on my works and deeds, they will spy on yours. They will always and everywhere be your opponents, because of me. It can happen that you will be dragged into the courts, thrown into prison, sent to exile — and they will even kill you, believing that they are doing God's work! I tell you all this so that when it happens you will remember; you can then say, 'He warned us well.' "

> These words are found in the Gospel of John, the end of chapter 15 and the beginning of chapter 16.

And in fact, all twelve of the companions who heard these words — and Matthias in Judas' place — would know martyrdom and would give their blood for the reign of God.

REFLECTIONS

As Long As You Love A Person Or Thing More Than You Love God, It Is Impossible To Be A Priest.

Even if God has willed to need men and thus calls them in spite of their faults and weaknesses, Christ cannot admit among his followers anyone who loves a creature, a person or a human goal more than they love him.

A priest is not by definition a husband and family head with a respectable reputation, or a loyal and conscientious businessman, or a builder of temples or showrooms, or a scholar versed in scientific research, or an almsgiver and social organizer, or an administrator competent in the exercise of his functions (even religious), or an organizer of recreation programs, a protector of the "good order" of society, a union leader, a well-meaning protester, etc., etc. The priest — as you have seen in the many preceding pages — is above all to be seen as a hostage taking the sin of the world upon himself in imitation of Christ, so that the world can be freed and humankind reestablished according to God's original plan: its complete fulfillment on a level with God himself.

As Don Bosco's mother said on the day of the ordination of this great saint and teacher in the church, "Learn, my son, that to begin saying Mass is to begin to suffer!"

A man once jeered at a totally selfless priest whose goodness was well-known that, "Every priest is still a man." The other responded, "A priest is the sacrifice of man joined to that of God. That is the priesthood."

You do not go into the priesthood in a state of naïve enthusiasm. It is not enough to be strongly moved to give yourself to the noblest and greatesy of causes. Beyond that, you must assume the burden of sin — and help Christ to carry his cross, as Simon of Cyrene did. No one rushes to proclaim himself a hostage while reciting stirring poetry or singing sentimental ballads.

***

1. Poverty

One of the first renunciations which must be accepted is the abandonment of money, the easy life, and comfort. The priesthood cannot be seen as a money-making

career where one makes his fortune, nor as a step up the social ladder which guarantees one's status.

No one denies that basic conditions of life and facilities for a fruitful apostolate are necessary.

But the priest, no less than anyone else, cannot serve both God and money, as Jesus said. And anyone who has ever tried to link these two has always ended up being ineffective, an obstacle to the reign of God, or simply a quitter. You can reread the pages above dealing with this "temptation" to advance the coming of God's reign by making compromises with money and comfort.

The priest needs to apply to himself the words the apostle Paul preached to the Thessalonians: "Have you ever seen me flatter anyone? Or preach for money? Ah! Never! I call God as a witness. Remember instead the crushing work we undertook. Laboring night and day to be a charge to no one among you. Paul was a tent weaver. We preached the gospel earning our own living. And yet we had the right to live from this ministry."

These words are found in the First Letter of Paul to the Christians at Thessalonika, chapter 2; and in his second letter, chapter 3.

Saying farewell to the Christians of Ephesus, Paul could write: "I desired neither gold nor silver. Look at these hands. You know it is by the fruit of my own labor that I wanted my companions and myself to live. And in this way too I also wanted to help the poor, remembering the saying of the Lord Jesus himself: 'It is better to give than to receive.'"

These words are found in the Book of the Acts of the Apostles, chapter 20 (verses 33 to 38).

***

2. Celibacy

Another renunciation necessary to becoming an apostle of Christ is that of starting a family. The Church requires its priests not to become married.

If we are looking seriously at the question of the priesthood, we must be honest with one another here. For you have undoubtedly already heard it said around you that such a requirement is tyrannical and represents an attack on man's liberty, the distrust of a great human value, an act of violence against nature and a danger to physical and emotional health — that such a renunciation renders a priest unable to deal with family and marital problems, makes him separate and soulless, incapable of understanding other men and women, his brothers and sisters.

You will not have allowed yourself to be unreasonably impressed by these arguments, for marriage and a family are not the only paths leading to the total fulfillment of the human person. Man is not flesh alone and the sexual instinct is not everything for him.

When he renounces the legitimate joys and family obligations of marriage, the future priest does not mean to register either his distrust of the gift of human life or his fear of social responsibilities — certainly not. But since he has been seized by Christ, he has chosen to keep all his affective strengths and capacity for action for him alone.

If the great love of a man for a woman is enough to explain his keeping his entire life for her alone — and we have the histories of explorers, sailors, prisoners, and others which tell us that men can remain chaste for long periods of time — that it is just as fitting, and noble and great that a man love God enough to consecrate his whole life to him, too.

This way the priest truly becomes a thing of God's, something like the cup consecrated for the eucharist which no longer serves any profane purpose, no matter how honorable. His celibacy becomes the visible sign of his total and irreversible gift in the eyes of all.

The witness of hundreds of thousands of men around the world living the fidelity of this total gift at this very moment is obviously impressive; all told, those who leave it behind are still the exception. This striking phenomenon is one proof of the reality of the reign of God at the heart of the world. We might ask who it is that can ask and receive such a gift of self from men. There is no one but Christ who can take a man in the fullness of his life and lift him out into an even wider reality. For it is sure that the heroism implied in such a total, exclusive and perpetual gift of self is beyond merely human strength. But this is one of the basic points of this book: the reign of God has its own hidden strength which can overturn the commonly accepted scale of values taken for granted in this world.

We should not be afraid to affirm that the priest bears witness in his commitment to chastity to a world to come — the new world of eternity where material joys will give way to satisfactions which are much more substantial and never disappointing. This world down here sings the charms and delights of human loving in its songs, films, drama, literature, and poetry — but it also makes plain to us the limits, illusions, pain, and regret of such loving. The priest giving up this carnal union is already a new man, already a citizen of the world to come, an anticipation of future humanity. At that time, on Jesus' own word, men and women will become sons and daughters of the resurrection, new immortal creatures; and there will no longer be husbands and wives among them, but all will know a wholly different and immeasurably more exalted life.

<small>These words are found in the Gospels of Matthew (chapter 22, verses 23 to 33) and Mark (chapter 12, verses 18 to 27).</small>

In addition, living as he does in chastity and outside the married state, the priest can give himself to others in a more universal way. You can give of your life much more freely when you don't have special duties to a home and loved ones. It's better that nothing stand in the priest's way as he tries to give his life, whether this be in a foreign place, with a people or tribe of another color, in the poorest and most desperate countries of the world, during outbreaks of war, persecution, and sickness, or in concentration or refugee camps. To be everything to everyone, to become this "broken bread" offered to all men and women, it is fitting that the priest give his heart to no one person. His role as intermediary between God and man, as confidant and confessor, makes it difficult to admit the intimate presence of a woman into his life. And the future he would have to assure for his children could easily lead him to serious compromise incompatible with his position. Finally, the argument that the priest would be more qualified to understand the persons confided to him if he were himself married is not as clear-cut as all that. The priest is not supposed to play the role of a professional marriage counselor; and even within a marriage, the husband himself cannot know everything there is to be known: he has not experienced the pain and anguish of his wife during childbirth, for example. The priest has already learned enough in his studies; and he lives in the world, not in some cloistered enclosure.

It is married Christians who must bear witness in the world about married life and family according to the law of Christ. On their marriage day the church recalls to them what Paul the apostle said to the first Christians, that their union should mirror the union between Christ and his church. For the covenant between Christ and his church was fulfilled in the blood of Calvary; Jesus went so far as to die for his church. In return the church gave itself to Christ in suffering martyrdom to remain faithful to him. When Paul said this to the first Christians, there were many who had chosen to die as the victims of persecution rather than renounce the commitment they made at baptism. So if the witness given by the Christian family to the world is that of an absolute faithfulness between husband and wife until death itself, the witness of the priest is that of a life given exclusively and until death in the service of Christ and his church.

These words of the apostle Paul are found in his Letter to the Christians at Ephesus, chapter 5 (verses 25 to 27).

It is true that Christ did not impose celibacy on his apostles or their successors. Peter and most of the others were married when they responded to his call. The apostle Paul states in his letters that he received no formal command from Christ about this; but he himself counseled chastity.

The celibacy of priests is a response to the requirements of the Christian community. It was in the fourth and fifth centuries that the laws of the church formalized the already ancient custom of choosing bishops only from among men committed to celibacy. And little by little it became normal to require priests, who assisted the bishops, to observe the same celibacy.

Taken in themselves, being a priest and being married are not irreconcilable states. So it is that in the Eastern churches, even those in communion with Rome, priests are permitted to marry; nonetheless, bishops are always celibate. The candidate for the priesthood chooses his way before he is ordained a priest: he either marries or commits himself to celibacy; but once ordained he can no longer marry.

As for the Western church, the Pope recently published an encyclical letter recalling the ancient practice of this discipline and explaining that celibacy was fitting as the proof of a greater love for God and humankind, and that it served as a kind of guarantee of apostolic freedom, allowing the priest to be more a "man for others." It is the church's obligation to set down the requirements for those who want to commit themselves to the priesthood.

This requirement can at times be felt as a burden by the priest and his solitude can weigh heavily on him, especially when he is confronted with a kind of distrust, hostility or defiance on the part of those around him. At these times he feels something of what it means to be "crucified" in following Christ, in being associated with the experience Jesus lived through. But when this happens, he can also say with the one who felt abandoned by all, "I am not alone, for my Father is with me."

> These words of Christ are found in the Gospel of John, chapter 8 (verses 28 and 29).

The solitude of the priest is never empty, so much is his heart filled with God and the wealth of his reign. We should also add that the priest receives a powerful support from the religious environment in which he lives, through his permanent contact with Christ in each day's eucharist, his life of prayer, and his ministry itself.

***

3. Life in Community.

There is another requirement for the priesthood which responds directly to the solitude he often feels: living in community, in a group. Let's stop to reflect on it a little.

We saw above that Christ wanted to gather his companions in a community, a group, a "church." These were the twelve companions closest to him, whom he made responsible for the spreading of the gospel throughout the world; but the twelve taken as a closely-knit group with Peter at the center. More than a symbol of unity, Peter was promoted to the role of "foundation-stone," assuring the solidity and cohesion of the whole structure; he was the keystone at the center of the vault which holds all the others in place and keeps them from collapsing. "Peter," Jesus said to him one day, "you strengthen your brother"; that is, build them up, bring them together, keep them from falling apart. When the other materials are not solidly linked to the foundation, the keystone, of a structure, faults begin to appear in the construction; collapse will soon follow. Some columns or stretches of wall might still stand, but they are disjointed; there is no longer any structure.

> These words of Christ to Peter are found in Luke's Gospel, chapter 22 (verses 31 and 32).

For this reason priests are required to live in community, in a group, united first of all to their bishop, then to other priests who assist the bishop in his apostolic labors. The preaching of the reign of God and the salvation of men in Christ can only be achieved at this price.

In twenty centuries of church history we have seen immense fissures — "schism" is another word for fissure — appear in the church because those who were responsible for the spread of the gospel and the salvation of men could not or would not understand one another, accept one another, love one another in the unity of this great body which has Christ as its head.

No one can hope to work for the reign of God while "doing his own thing" or going about his own separate way. For you have probably noticed already that one of the most difficult things in the world is for a man to give up his own private freedom to live out his own illusions. People are sometimes more concerned with their own ideas, their own ways of seeing, judging and acting than with family ties. They are ready to offer their lives, but they recognize no control; they intend to row their own boat, at the same time working for the reign of God. But in doing so they risk becoming all wrapped up in themselves and cutting themselves off from God. This is why a man who aims for the priesthood is required to commit himself on the path of obedience to the church of Christ where Jesus remains in active presence, guarding it from all serious error.

This account is found in the Letter of the apostle Paul to the Christians at Galatia, chapters 1 and 2.

It is fitting to illustrate this with a magnificent example. Paul the apostle, whose conversion you read about above, explained in a letter to the Christians at Galatia how he had made a point of meeting with James and Peter before beginning to proclaim the gospel, even though he had already been directly instructed through special revelation from Christ. Later, having gone all over the Mediterranean preaching Christ, he returned to Jerusalem to look for James, Peter, and John in order to have his teaching approved: "I wanted their assurance," he wrote, "that I had not undertaken all my missionary work in vain. For these authorities in the church, who are rightly known as the pillars of Christianity, impose nothing new. They recognized that my vocation was truly to preach the gospel among the pagans, just as Peter had received the mission to preach it among the Jews. They bound me only to remember the poor Christians in Jerusalem and to help them by organizing some collections — something which I have never forgotten to do."

This excerpt from Paul brings out all the richness, diversity, effectiveness and certainty of life in a group, in community. Each one complements the other. In our day when life is more and more complex, when different cultures and civilizations meet and exchange with increasing depth, we cannot hope to spread the gospel without possessing a team spirit, an ability to work in a group with others. Everyone has his own gifts, his "charisms" for meeting and sharing with different people and for adapting to different mentalities. Paul explained this to the Christians of Corinth one day: "There are many kinds of spiritual gifts, but they all come from the same spirit. There are all kinds of functions and services in the church, but they all refer to the same Lord. And these gifts and favors are given for the good of all: one has the gift to really understand religion, another to bring it to people; one has such trust in God that he does marvels, another has the gift to help the sick; one is a contemplative who raises his inspired prayers to God, another has a gift of leadership and is able to direct the local church."

In our day this can mean that one person is competent in teaching Christian doctrine as a professor in a seminary, while another is made for leading a parish, a Catholic Action group, or a diocese; one has a gift for catechetical work with children, another for preparing young people for marriage, and yet another for presiding over liturgical celebrations. One might find his place in an apostolate among the middle class and well-to-do, while another is effective in a working-class neighborhood. One person could be influential on a professional level in the economic, social or even international field, another a worker among the poor, oppressed and despised. One is dedicated to working with young people in vocational schools, another to serving among the elderly and handicapped. One priest will give witness in the workplace, the factory, or the office, while his brother labors among engineers and technicians in a research center. One could be a union or political organizer, the other will have a gift with the masses... and so on.

But as Paul said, "it is always one and the same spirit, the spirit of Christ working in each one and distributing his gifts as he wills. Look at the human body: it

Paul's whole development of this theme can be found in his First Letter to the Christians at Corinth, chapter 12.

brings together in a unity all its different members in order to form one single organism. And yet the hand is not a foot and the eye is not an ear. What if the foot were to say, 'I am not a hand, so I am not a part of the body'; would it cease to be part of the body in reality? If the whole body were an eye, what would do the work of the ear? The eye cannot say to the hand, 'I have no use for you,' nor the head to the feet, 'I can get along without you.' Does one member suffer? All the others suffer with it. The whole body is plunged into suffering. Does one member of the body receive praise? All the others take part in its joy. It is the whole body that is happy."

Likewise, the more a priestly community united to its bishop is rich in its diversity of gifts, the greater is the personal fulfillment of each of its members. And the more the reign of God will be spread on earth and salvation in Jesus Christ communicated to men.

But this life in community which is so important in the life of the priest, assuring his fulfillment and broadening his possibilities, obviously requires a certain amount of renunciation.

There is certainly the question of temperament. It is sometimes difficult to adapt to this law of group living: "to accept one another as different and love one another as complementary." (You should note that this is the first rule of marriage, too: lifelong group living between two people.)

We encounter some examples of this difficulty in the life of Paul the apostle. Barnaby was one of his best friends. It was Barnaby who introduced the converted Paul to the community of the first Christians in Jerusalem. Together they had organized the first great missionary voyage throughout the Mediterranean region. Later they came back to Antioch. In no time Paul began talking of going back on another trip to see how the young communities they had founded were getting along. Barnaby agreed, but on the condition that they take Mark along, as they did on their first trip. But Paul was against it: Mark had abandoned them at Pamphyliae at the most dangerous point of their mission, when they had to go through real bandit territory in the Taurus mountains; he went back to Jerusalem and stayed with his widowed mother. Paul judged that Mark (who would later write a gospel) lacked physical stamina and didn't have a character tough enough or a spirit lively enough to suit the life of a missionary. Barnaby would not give in; at other times he had always yielded before the more dominant personality of Paul in the group, but now he found the other too severe. He had every reason to believe that

This account is found in the Book of the Acts of the Apostles, chapter 15 (verses 36 to 40).

Mark would be more helpful and more courageous in the future. Paul grew obstinate; he wanted to give this young slacker a lesson he would never forget. The discussion became heated, and ended up in a break. Paul and Barnaby could no longer see eye-to-eye and had to split up. Barnaby, friend from first, the truly faithful companion, would not let go this time. Paul, too, remained inflexible; he had decided Mark would not go along, and he started a new group with Luke and Sylvain. And things were better this way; the saints were still men and the apostolic work was not accomplished in an atmosphere of clashing temperaments. Yet Barnaby saw better than Paul the situation here, and the future would prove him right. Mark would end up overcoming his timid and fearful temperament; he would become very effective in spreading the gospel. And Paul himself would recognize this. Later on, they would work together in Rome. It was in instances like this that the common goal these men shared in Christ brought them to finally overcome interpersonal problems.

Another requirement of group living is the common sharing of each person's views and positions concerning apostolic life. Community living and teamwork presuppose that each person speak his mind, that no one try to avoid the issue but lay his cards on the table in all simplicity — his ideas, his convictions, his commitments — and that each one accept the fraternal criticism of the others; in short, that he make known to the others in all charity what he thinks of their way of seeing, judging, and acting upon the issues and situations they all face. This is called "revision of life."

It is certainly a worthwhile renunciation to refuse to be your own self-appointed judge and to accept criticism and even correction at times; this is part of the spirit of poverty mentioned above which consists not only in detachment from material riches, but also in listening, understanding, being receptive, knowing your own limits. There is less of a risk of going astray while seeking a goal as important as the salvation of men and women; this is why "revision of life" implies such great advantages.

It is true that apart from fundamental religious truths there is freedom of opinion in the church, and priests, like all Christians, maintain their critical sense in a context of love and mutual respect. This freedom is very important: men and women in the church can have different points of view, different ways of acting in matters that have not been defined once and for all. Furthermore, this diversity of opinion and action is often a means to arrive at a clearer picture of controversial situations and thus to move ahead more surely.

But in a priestly community — and this is equally true in a Christian household between husband and wife — one should also know how to carry out a revision of life in a context of mutual understanding and fraternal love.

We find an admirable example of this in the book of the Acts of the Apostles. At one point the apostle Paul came into a disagreement with Peter over a question of the method of conducting the apostolate which seemed to place the purity of the gospel message in jeopardy. First of all, Peter, in a famous vision on the roof of a house in Joppa which had a great view of the river and the wide sea, understood that after Christ there was no privileged race. All peoples were united and joined by the blood of Christ which flowed from the cross. The Jewish law had found its fulfillment in Christ; now its mission was completed. Pagans, who had never known the ancient law of Moses, could now enter the church directly through baptism without first converting to Judaism. Belonging to Christ was enough to be a part of the people of God. On the strength of these reflections inspired by the Holy Spirit, the helmsman of the church cast off his lines and set sail for the wide seas. He accepted Roman families into baptism. But little by little, under the influence of communities of Jews who had converted to Christ, he allowed himself to make certain concessions and began to make distinctions between pagans who had received baptism directly and those

This account is found in the Book of the Acts of the Apostles, chapter 10.

who had first accepted the law of Moses.

It was at this point that Paul protested loudly and brought Peter to account before everyone: "If, after having sought the true meaning of life in our adhesion to Christ, we now judge that that is not enough and that we still have to return to the regulations of the Jewish law then we are really saying that we judge Christ incapable of making us saints. God forbid that we do so!" The point was to tell Peter that his behavior could be badly interpreted.

This account is found in the Letter of Paul to the Christians at Galatia, chapter 2 (verses 11 and following).

Instead of balking and using his position as leader to silence Paul, Peter understood that his attitude could be misjudged and made an effort to correct this.

Community living and teamwork among Christ's apostles, you see, is all of that.

In our day it is hard to see how a priest could, practically speaking, live and work alone and isolated. The priest is always closely linked not only to his bishop but also to a group of other priests who work in the same city, the same region, or the same apostolate. This assures fraternal support, mutual enrichment, some control, surer doctrine and greater effectiveness in the apostolate.

Beginning in the seminary, those who are getting ready for the priesthood lead a community life which opens them out to others and brings them personal fulfillment. As you have seen, this implies certain demands on their lifestyle. It is always in deciding to carry one's own cross that one begins to follow Christ.

***

4. A Life Given Without Reserve.

Like the other companions, Peter and Paul were to take their gift of self to the extreme of martyrdom.

Looking back over his adventurous life totally dedicated to God's work — and the life of every priest is an adventure, for the greatest risks are taken by those who commit themselves — Paul gave this brief account in a letter to the Christians in Corinth:

"In my life I have undertaken much work for the gospel. I have often been sent to prison, whipped to the point of death many times. Five times I received the thirty-nine lashes before the Jewish tribunals, and three times I was whipped by the Romans. One day I was even stoned and left for dead (it was at Lystra). I was shipwrecked three times and once adrift in the open sea for a night and a day. I have made countless voyages and I ran the worst dangers: danger from rivers, from outlaws, danger from my own people and from pagans; I was in danger in the cities, in the lonely deserts, in danger from the sea and in danger from so-called brothers. I often spent long nights without sleep, without food or drink, without warmth. And without going into detail, there is the crushing responsibility I must bear each day, my anguished care for all the communities I have founded. When any man has suffered, I have suffered; when any one of them has fallen, I have been moved by a passionate desire to save them... .

"I would never finish telling my whole story; there were even less striking moments. One day, at Damascus, the whole city was placed on the alert for me; I had to be let down over the walls in a basket, through a window, in order to escape.

"But the Lord has always strengthened me. And I could even boast of the marvelous revelations he has granted me; yet I prefer to boast of my weaknesses, of the physical weaknesses I must endure which are like a blow from Satan for me; they keep me from getting too proud. I asked the Lord to stop these trials; he made me understand that his grace is enough and that his power shines forth all the better out of the weaknesses of men. So I am happy to accept my infirmities since the power of Christ shows through them all the more clearly. I can even rejoice at all that happens to me: sickness, insults, abandonment, hardships, anguish, and persecution; I bear them for Christ's sake, because when I am weak is when I am really strong."

Paul would finish his life imprisoned in Rome and would be beheaded; likewise with Peter, who would be

This account is found in the Second Letter of the apostle Paul to the Christians at Corinth, chapters 11 and 12.

tortured to death at the same time in the same city. But it was from Rome that the religion of Christ would spread throughout the whole world.

It would take too long to recount here the story of how twenty centuries of men and women dedicated to the service of Christ have given their lives in martyrdom and persecution. The history of the Church is woven of these lives given in blood. Martyr-priests must be counted in the thousands. But there are also countless priests who have given the whole of their lives without being led to the brutal step of martyrdom, who have served Christ every day of their lives in giving themselves freely for the salvation of men. "There is no greater love," Jesus said, "than to lay down your life for those you love."

chapter four
The Joy in Jesus' Call

Real happiness? A hundred times over! Beginning even in this life for those who put their trust in God and follow his Christ.

One day Peter, in the name of all the companions and in face of all the renunciations which flowed from their decision to follow Jesus, put this question to him in all trust: "All told, we have left everything to follow you. What will we receive in return?"

Peter had not yet been transformed; he was still very down-to-earth in his way of seeing things. Jesus accepted him for what he was and said, "Wait until the time of new life in the future world; you will know a glorious life at my side. To give you an idea of what that will be, imagine the leaders of your people in all the splendor of their thrones."

This episode is found in the Gospels of Mark (chapter 10, verses 18 to 31) and Luke (chapter 18, verses 28 to 30).

And he added, "So it will be for all those who have left their goods, their houses and fields; who have renounced their family life, agreed to have neither wife nor children, and all for the sake of the gospel, to proclaim the reign of God.

"But I tell you that even in this very life they will discover a hundred times more happiness than all those things would have brought them."

What was that? The satisfaction of riches, a good reputation, a comfortable life, good contacts, influence and power — a hundred times better!

What else? The legitimate pleasures of marriage, the joy and responsibility of fatherhood, the happiness of human affection — a hundred times more!

And Jesus said again, "These people will be happy even in the midst of persecution." This is how much they will feel that their life has a meaning, that it's going somewhere. Thus, those who have "played God's game" will know an immense happiness, even in this life.

Moreover, Peter would solemnly affirm this on the day that Jesus multiplied the bread to feed the hungry crowds. Following a talk in which he announced that from now on the true bread of life was himself, that his flesh and blood would be the food which would guarantee man's reconciliation with God and immortality, Jesus saw that his listeners found his words difficult to understand and that they went away disappointed in their hope to find in him a leader to win them bread and liberation. He then asked his twelve closest companions, "And you; will you also leave me?" At that point Peter understood that his life would no longer have any meaning if he left Christ after so many eventful weeks together, and he answered for himself and all the others, "But where would we go? You alone have the secret of true life, the words of eternal life."

Peter's response to Jesus is found in John's Gospel, chapter 6 (verses 60 to 71).

REFLECTIONS

Christ is the only historical personage to whom men still give their lives... twenty centuries after his appearance on earth.

You have surely asked yourself, dear reader, at one time or another in your life, if Christ was really God.

Among other proofs, it has been pointed out that he was the only figure in history who dared to make such an exorbitant claim. He did so on many occasions. Yet the other great leaders of the world religions — like Confucius, Buddha and Mohammed — never made a similar declaration or stated such a claim.

In concluding these pages, I would like to put this observation into context by underlining the amazing fact that Jesus is the only figure in the history of man who continues to be loved twenty centuries after men saw him on earth. The great men and famous conquerors, striking men of genius, artists, poets, philosophers, and all the great benefactors of humanity — men like Alexander, Caesar, Napoleon, Socrates, Plato, Michelangelo, Beethoven, Lincoln, Einstein, Karl Marx, and so many others — these men have found a place of admiration and recognition among many peoples.

But who loves them?

Love is different from admiration and recognition. To love someone is to feel attracted to them, to want to live in their presence, live only for them, forget the cost in trying to please them, accept all kinds of difficulties and suffering for their sake — in short, to love someone is to give them your life. Young people getting married, older couples with homes and families, mothers with their infants — all can attest that love is something more than admiration and recognition.

The great men of the past find no place in our hearts. They mean little in our lives. But Christ — he who won no great battles, who brought no new inventions to light, who left no musical or artistic masterpieces — this Christ is still so loved after twenty centuries that millions of men and women give him their life. He foretold it well: "When I have been lifted up from the earth on the cross, then I will attract a world to me; it is then that I will turn all hearts to me!"

Many great men — heroes, artists, athletes, singers — excited much enthusiasm in their contemporaries. They were once loved. While they are still living they might continue to provoke passionate acclaim. It is said that some of Napoleon's soldiers were once driven by such frenzy that they gave their life for their chief and died crying, "Long live the emperor!" And the same madness drove some of Hitler's troops. But this sort of thing lasts no longer than the "idol" in question. Once their followers are dead and their power has been divided up — often amidst bloody intrigues — history takes over and consigns their memory to criticism, distrust, abandonment, and, often, scorn.

In contrast, millions of men and women of all ages from every country, every race, every culture and every social condition have never seen Christ and yet still prove their love for him after twenty centuries.

Isn't this the greatest proof that Christ still lives and that he is the Son of God? To turn men's hearts after twenty centuries — what man could boast so much?

Friend, as I finish these pages, I want to express my wish that your heart be turned and seized by him, so much so that you will hear his call and walk after him. Others, men who have been given the responsibility to talk with young men like yourself about the apostolic life, will counsel you in your search and will tell you if you really can be a priest. Only, don't think that you will be throwing your life away — just the opposite: this is a way your life might succeed beyond your wildest dreams. Beginning right here in your own life you will know the hidden and liberating joy of being in Christ's service for the salvation and transfiguration of humanity.

In place of a signature here, I, the author, would like to tell you who have made the effort to read right up to these last lines, that I have been a priest for over thirty years now; and in spite of the problems and shadows which are part of all human life, I have never regretted one day of my priesthood.